becoming
BARNABAS

PAUL MOOTS

becoming BARNABAS

THE MINISTRY OF ENCOURAGEMENT

THE ALBAN INSTITUTE

HERNDON, VIRGINIA

www.alban.org

Scripture quotations, unless otherwise noted, are from *The New Jerusalem Bible*, copyright © 1966 by Darton, Longman & Todd, Ltd., and Doubleday & Company, Inc. Used by permission of the publisher.

Scripture quotations marked "NIV" are from HOLY BIBLE, New International Version, copyright © 1973, 1978, 1984. Used by permission of Zondervan Bible Publishers.

Cover design: Adele Robey, Phoenix Graphics
Cover art: Photo detail of stained glass window, "St. Barnabas," designed, painted, and fabricated by Scotty Giffen, stained glass artist, for St. Barnabas Church, London Ontario. Copyright © Scotty Giffen. Photographed by Scotty Giffen. Mr. Giffen continues to create stained glass works of art and may be contacted at scottygiffen_usa@hotmail.com

Library of Congress Cataloging-in-Publication Data

Moots, Paul.
  Becoming Barnabas : the ministry of encouragement / Paul Moots.
    p. cm.
  Includes bibliographical references (p.   ).
  ISBN 1-56699-293-1
    1. Christian leadership. 2. Barnabas, Apostle, Saint. 3. Encouragement—Religious aspects—Christianity. I. Title.
  BV652.1.M66 2004
  253—dc22
                                                    2004005851

08   07   06   05   04   VG   1   2   3   4   5   6   7   8   9   10

CONTENTS

FOREWORD

HOW TO GROW, FIX, OR SAVE YOUR CONGREGATION is the topic of more books than anyone of us probably cares to read. Many are simplistic, if not instrumentalist, and promise far more than the authors can ever deliver or the readers can carry out. As a result, people often become discouraged and resigned to the way things are or spend much time trying out every new method and technique that come along to revitalize their congregations.

In *Becoming Barnabas*, Paul Moots challenges us to a "ministry of encouragement" that is rooted in an understanding and imagining of the life and work of Barnabas, a minor but influential character in the book of Acts, and in his own experience as a pastor in different settings over the past 22 years.

Early on, Moots makes it clear that every congregation has a unique story—its own history, culture, make-up, life, and ministry. Understanding each congregation takes time and energy, and there are no short cuts to faithfulness. Unfortunately, many of us have been succumbed to the allure of short cuts and have hurried off to workshops, devoured the latest books on church life, and rushed "to duplicate their strategies without considering their rightness for our own setting and without preparing the congregations we serve for the changes these strategies will require" (p. xii).

When studying and preaching through the books of Acts, however, Moots's attention was increasingly drawn to the role and personality of Barnabas and how he embodies a ministry of encouragement. When so many changes are going on in the larger society and church, and congregations are buffeted by so many conflicting views within and without, the ministry of Barnabas offers a helpful perspective for our own work and provides an apt metaphor for our times.

The book is structured around different experiences of encouragement that Moots has discovered, both by mining biblical texts about Barnabas and by wrestling in a transparent and compelling manner with his own life and ministry. For him the ministry of encouragement involves partnership, hospitality, courage, reconciliation, character, and call. All of these qualities are found in different experiences of Barnabas in his ministry in the early church. Moots argues that these qualities are desperately needed today.

In the latter part of the book we are reminded that ministry is a process "that will differ from church to church and individual to individual rather than a one-size-fits-all program" (p. 112). Moots's commitment to this principle is one of the major strengths of the book. As communities of faith, we are always in the process of becoming; we are always Christians-in-training. There are no ready-made answers. We will make mistakes, be trapped by old habits, resist new challenges, and forget to pray for the Spirit's guidance. Yet God promises to be with us by doing new things, taking us to new places, and encouraging us always through the life of the Spirit.

Becoming Barnabas is not a book just for clergy. It is really directed to all of us, the people of God, who are called together into ministry. This point is emphasized again and again. The ministry of encouragement involves the entire congregation. Each of us has gifts to offer, and the challenge is to call forth and affirm the gifts of one another. The church can become a liberating and transforming community of faith that validates our diverse ministries as God's people day in and day out. However, as Moots points out, we will not become such communities unless we are intentional in our efforts and determined that our congregations will become places that send us forth again and again to carry out a ministry of encouragement wherever we find ourselves.

Moots takes us beyond his book by pointing to many resources along the way. Chapters are rich with biblical and theological references that may be helpful to the reader in exploring more broadly various aspects and challenges of church life today. He includes writers with different perspectives and insights, even conflicting ones. The last chapter of the book ends with an annotated bibliography of books that Moots has found helpful in formulating his own views about a ministry of encouragement.

Finally, we are confronted with questions about congregational life and ministry that ask us to engage in serious reflection. Moots wants us to participate in the journey, to be actively engaged in our different contexts, to be part of the process. Moots offers no blueprints for success but the promise that we are not alone and that Barnabas can serve as a mentor for many of us. Moots concludes that "our legacy will be in the ministries of the churches we have served and those whose ministry we have stimulated and supported" (p. 127). In this time of great turmoil and anguish in society and many congregations, Moots offers much encouragement to pastors and church leaders who seek to be faithful to God's continuing call and to flourish in the life of the Spirit.

Robert Reber
Center for Christian Leadership
Methodist Theological School, Ohio

PREFACE

Why Barnabas?

There was a Levite of Cypriot origin called Joseph whom the disciples surnamed Barnabas (which means "son of encouragement").—Acts 4:36

YOUR MAIL—OR YOUR PASTOR'S—probably looks much like mine. In the past two weeks I have received several pieces aimed at helping me grow in ministry—invitations to a national convocation on evangelism, an institute of parish ministry, and a church-growth seminar, to pick just three. Each lists an impressive array of instructors and motivators. Speaking at all three events is Michael Slaughter, who has led Ginghamsburg United Methodist Church in Tipp City, Ohio, through a transformation from a small country congregation into a vital church of more than 2,000 members. Bill Hybels of Willow Creek Ministries (South Barrington, Illinois) and Rick Warren of Saddleback Community Church, Lake Forest, California, are leaders at two of these events, as is Kirbyjon Caldwell, pastor of the fastest-growing United Methodist congregation in the United States (Windsor Village UMC, Houston). Other leaders, though perhaps less well known than these, are described in the brochures as pastors of churches that have multiplied in membership by several times in a single generation.

Much can be learned from these church leaders. They have rediscovered the power of small groups in building a vital congregation. They have used new technologies both to present the gospel in new and exciting ways and to reach spiritual seekers who would not respond to "church as usual." Some of their congregations have grown by reaching out to groups treated as untouchable by other churches or by ignoring common wisdom about the lack of viability of multiracial congregations. (Jim Cymbala of Brooklyn [New York] Tabernacle and Cecil Williams, who revitalized Glide Memorial United Methodist, San Francisco, come to mind in this category.) We can learn much from their commitment and witness, the curricula and methods they have developed, their openness to change, and their flexibility and willingness to risk failure to follow the gospel.

There is a downside, though, to turning only to these leaders and those of other large churches as our models for ministry. It is no secret that Western culture has made a cult of success, and that success American-style is couched in terms of size or growth or wealth or winning. The danger is that the church has accepted the larger culture's definition by regarding success as growth in membership size and budget, rather than as faithfulness in discipleship. Too many of us in parish ministry attend these workshops, read books by their leaders, and rush to duplicate their strategies without considering their rightness for our own setting and without preparing the congregations we serve for the changes these strategies will require. With visions of leading the next megachurch dancing in our heads, we too often discover that we cannot duplicate the success of these churches in our current context. (Note that I do not say "with our current congregations." Congregations in a variety of settings and circumstances can and do make changes to strengthen their ministry. However, pastors impatient for results too often simply neglect the task of preparing for change and then blame the congregation when change is resisted. We do not ready the context for success.) We become discouraged, disillusioned, and perhaps even envious. As pastoral theologian Eugene Peterson outlines in his superb book *Under the Unpredictable Plant,* we are too often Jonahs yearning for the unlimited possibilities for ministry in Tarshish, rather than the dull routine and deaf ears we expect to find in Nineveh.[1] Wishing to be elsewhere is not the way to serve one of Christ's congregations. Not all of our churches will become megachurches, nor should they. Many will not become successful by the standards of our culture. This does not mean that they cannot accomplish vital ministry, nor does it mean that they have failed in discipleship to Christ. There is still a role for medium-size and small congregations. Kennon Callahan, whose work on church growth has helped start and build many megacongregations, addresses this reality in his book *Small, Strong Congregations.* Callahan says he believes that in the 21st century "more people will be drawn to small, strong congregations than [to] any other kind."[2] At their best, the strengths of small, strong congregations lie in their intimacy and shared history, their sense of compassion and mission, and their self-reliance and generosity. While these strengths also exist in many large congregations, they are most often cultivated in large churches that have consciously organized themselves as a number of smaller communities within the larger. "The truth," says Callahan, "is that bigger is bigger, not necessarily better. The truth is that smaller is smaller, not necessarily better. . . . Small does small very, very well. Small does not try to do 'mini-mega.'"[3]

Despite all the current emphasis on using electronic media in worship, not every Christian or every seeker will hear the word of Christ in the click of the PowerPoint presentation or the electronic melodies of contemporary Christian music. As the writings of Kathleen Norris and Anne Lamott remind us, the traditional foundations of faith and worship remain powerful for many Christians *and seekers* even in the 21st century.

A word of introduction for those who have not encountered these remarkable writers and witnesses: Kathleen Norris speaks of her "reconversion." She grew up in the church but, like many young adults, drifted away in college. When, as an adult, she returned to the home her grandparents had built in South Dakota, she began to attend ("put on") her grandmother's church. The struggle of praying and working in community reawakened Norris's faith. She has invited us on her journey back to traditional Christianity—which includes a deep relationship with a Benedictine community as well as her Presbyterian congregation—in her books *Dakota, The Cloister Walk,* and *Amazing Grace.*[4]

Anne Lamott's witness is very different. She describes her conversion as a series of "staggers" toward God. Having overcome addiction and a series of painful affairs, and blessed by the birth of her son, Sam, Lamott found a home in an inner-city congregation. Like Norris, Lamott was healed through the shared struggles of a gracious community. Her faith story is a subtext of her books *Operating Instructions* and *Bird by Bird.* Her discovery of light in the darkest part of ordinary life is told in *Traveling Mercies.*[5] Although the circumstances of their journeys differed starkly, Norris and Lamott share the enduring value they found in Christian community and the touching and healing of their untraditional lives by theology and worship deeply rooted in tradition.

Although we can learn from the leaders mentioned in the opening paragraphs, we are not called to make our congregations into cookie-cutter versions of Willow Creek or Ginghamsburg. What we *are* called to remember is that every church can and must hear Jesus' mandate to make disciples of all nations and, by extension, to make disciples in all communities and congregations. All Christians can and must be challenged to make full use of our gifts in Christ's service. Regardless of size or liturgy or music style, every local church that faithfully follows Christ will see signs of spiritual growth and often numeric growth as well. With proper preparation and focus, every partnership between pastor and congregation should result in a challenging and fruitful ministry. What is often missing from these partnerships is attention to that phrase "with proper preparation and focus." It is precisely this point at which so many of us in the local church flounder: How do we both challenge the congregations in which we worship and serve to a deeper ministry, and—perhaps more problematic—how do we support our congregations in such a ministry? Where might we find a model to help us stimulate and challenge congregations that have difficulty understanding our common call to discipleship, as well as those that are motivated for ministry but unable to discern clearly God's specific call to them?

In each of my last two clergy appointments, I have taken a portion of my first year with the congregation to preach through the book of Acts. Following the story of the early church helps us consider just what the task of our own congregation is to be. It also raises questions about our own priorities for ministry. Both times I have preached such a series, the role and personality of Barnabas have caught my attention. His work is vital in the story of the early church's growth, although his contribution is often overshadowed in readers' minds by the two giants of Acts, Peter and Paul (whose potential for ministry Barnabas recognized and encouraged). The more I considered his work, the more Barnabas' example offered insight into my role as pastor. Barnabas personifies the ministry of encouragement.

I have selected five moments from Barnabas' ministry that illustrate what I mean by the ministry of encouragement. They do not cover all we can learn from Barnabas, but they do provide a starting point to explore encouragement and how it can work in ministry. The ministry of partnership is the subject of chapter 2, along with the theme of standing aside to further the ministry of another. Chapter 3 looks at the ministry of hospitality, of standing with others, particularly outsiders, in their search to follow Christ. In a church whose decisions too often seem motivated by fear—fear of change, fear of the "other," fear of failure—the theme of chapter 4 needs to be heard: standing against fear. Chapter 5 concerns the ministry of the second chance, a ministry Barnabas fulfills with both Saul and John Mark. In chapter 6 we look at issues of integrity—how we prepare ourselves to serve in the ministry of encouragement by attending to God's call and guidance. Finally, I conclude with some updates—both joys and "speed bumps"—on how the practice of this ministry has been developing within the congregation I now serve.

A word about method is appropriate here. Barnabas is an influential but minor character in Luke's narrative; a few dozen verses tell his story. I have added to this story through imagination and induction, and parts of my scriptural exposition reflect this. I have done my best to keep this speculation honest by checking it against the commentaries and other tools I used in researching Barnabas and his time. I hope my exploration of Barnabas' ministry is understood as being grounded in research and not simply in my own imagination and prejudice. Where I differ from prevailing opinion, the responsibility is mine and no one else's. I will do my best to signal the reader at points where the train of thought is my interpretation of Scripture rather than Scripture itself.

All biblical quotations are from the New Jerusalem Bible. I have chosen this less familiar translation because I believe familiarity with certain readings of Scripture can dull our ability to hear new insights that even the most familiar passage could offer us. I recommend reading this book with your own Bible open to the book of Acts, preferably in a translation new to you. It is also worth noting that, when I use examples involving people and congregations outside my personal experience, I have altered names and made cosmetic changes to some of the circumstances to protect confidentiality.

Although the majority of contemporary examples I use are based on incidents in churches where I have served or am serving, I cannot claim to be an untainted exemplar of the ministry of encouragement. I am still trying to shed the training I received in the CEO style of ministry from seminary and the pastors of my youth, and I often have to rediscipline and rededicate myself to Barnabas' way. Churches that knew me early in my ministry may be startled to read the words that follow. The fact is that the congregations where I have tried to live out Barnabas' ministry have so far fallen short of Willow Creek-like growth. The church where I now serve is working with me to discern and fulfill our shared ministry using Barnabas and his gift of encouragement as our models. We have had modest growth in membership, giving, and worship attendance, but we still find ourselves having to remind one another what we are trying to accomplish and in whose name we live and serve. We have seen significant victories. We are experiencing more depth in our prayer together. The number of people active in study and in ministry both inside and outside our church walls has grown. New people are mixing into the leadership. All these elements create a wonderful stew of energy and struggle. We are a work in progress.

The ministry of encouragement offers a workable pattern for church leadership, and it is effective. In any church where spiritual as well as numeric growth is happening, this ministry of encouragement is being exercised, even if it is called by a different name. I am convinced that accepting Barnabas as my model has changed my ministry for the better and that Barnabas' example can benefit any pastor and congregation who take his lessons seriously. While the chapters that follow were written from a pastor's point of view, I believe that lay leaders will also benefit from understanding and accepting the ministry of encouragement. In fact, my experience suggests that laity may initially be more open to this ministry than pastors and that many are already engaged in this ministry, whether consciously or not. I hope that pastors and lay leaders will study this book together as a way to evaluate their common ministry in Christ.

In an article published in *Leadership* magazine (Fall 2000), Sam Williams, who retired from pastoral ministry in San Diego to teach leadership and church planting at Golden Gate Baptist Seminary in Mill Valley, California, looks at the changes that have taken place in his 35 years of ministry and asserts:

> Discipleship has shifted from taking everyone through an identical process of classes and workbooks to the dynamic experience of uniquely and personally building spiritual truth into people's lives. It's harder, messier, and difficult to measure; but it's more effective in a culture that needs relationship more than certificates.[6]

Barnabas and his ministry of encouragement offer us a focus for this vital, messy, and exhilarating work.

Acknowledgments

Many people have helped me in the writing of this book. My thanks begin with the people of the four congregations that have educated me as I have tried to serve as their pastor: Grace United Methodist of Zanesville, Ohio; Summit United Methodist and Linden United Methodist of Columbus, Ohio; and above all, the people of First United Methodist of Mount Sterling, Ohio, who have offered me unquestioning support as I wrote these words. I am also grateful to the congregation that nurtured me as a child and teenager and gave me my first understanding of what church is, Zanesfield (Ohio) United Methodist Church. I also thank those who read the manuscript in its early form, particularly those who not only read but also offered advice and counsel: my brother, Philip Moots; clergy colleagues Alan Sippel, John Edgar, Wayne Clark, Sharon Hausman, Sue McClelland, Ray Lynn Schlief; and lay advisors Carolyn Forrest, Robin Liff, Keith Deel, Lynne Brown, and Sue Schoener. I thank my sermon-shaping groups for talking through the implications of Barnabas' ministry with me before I began to write. I appreciate my counselor, George Winter, whose wisdom and support helped me through the ending of a marriage and the shedding of an addiction, not to mention the writing of this book. I am grateful to Ian and Yvonne Martin for offering me refuge at the White Oak Inn in Danville, Ohio, as I did my initial work on this manuscript; to Pat and Bob Arbegast for their timely offer of a place of retreat; and to the staff and customers of Nora's Coffee Shop in Grove City, Ohio, who gave me a not-*too*-quiet place to write, protected my space, and acted as cheering section as I finished and submitted my manuscript.

Finally, I thank David Lott, Simon Hyoun, and the rest of the staff of the Alban Institute for their affirmation and support. My editor, Beth Gaede, and my copy editor, Jean Caffey Lyles, have been invaluable to my finished work. They accepted no vague or sloppy writing—of which there was a dismaying amount. In particular, Beth's suggestions for ways to expand my vision and improve my expression were always on-target and challenging. I am deeply in her debt.

This book is dedicated to my parents.

ONE

The Ministry of Encouragement

WHAT IS THE MINISTRY OF ENCOURAGEMENT? In his survey *Rediscovering Our Spiritual Gifts,* Charles V. Bryant,[1] a national and interdenominational workshop leader in the ministry of discovering and developing spiritual gifts, properly calls the gift "exhortation," although in this book I will use the word given in most current biblical translations, "encouragement." "Exhortation" derives from the Greek *paraklesis,* a close relative of *paraclete,* one New Testament name for the Holy Spirit. When John's Gospel speaks of the Spirit as "Paraclete," the writer is describing our experience of the Spirit as our "comforter" or "close companion." Bryant defines the gift of exhortation as "the extraordinary ability to *inspire, encourage, and strengthen* others in and through their efforts to live out God's will and calling as Christians in pain and pleasure, want and plenty." (italics added).[2] In a ministry of encouragement, we will stand by others, guide and counsel them, urge, comfort, motivate, strengthen, inspire, and console. Not surprisingly, Barnabas ("Barnabas,"

1

meaning "son of encouragement," is the name given by his co-workers to Joseph of Cyprus) is one of Bryant's prime examples of this spiritual gift. Bryant cites three incidents from Barnabas' ministry in his essay on exhortation—his act of giving in Acts 4:36-7, his recruitment of Saul as partner in ministry to Antioch (Acts 11:25-6), and his support for John Mark after the younger man is rejected by Paul (Acts 15:36-40).

The first of these is a simple act of stewardship and sharing. Barnabas sells a piece of land he owns and donates the proceeds to the church to be used for the care of the poor and widowed. Luke contrasts this act of generosity and the inspiration it brings the church with the halfhearted commitment and dishonesty of Ananias and Sapphira, a story told by Luke in the following chapter. In the second incident, Barnabas is asked to help in the growth of a new congregation in Antioch. Rather than attempt the task alone, he invites Saul, whom he has previously sponsored as a fellow worker for Christ, to join him; both the disciples in Antioch and Saul and Barnabas themselves grow in ministry through this invitation. We will look also at this second incident in more detail in chapter 2. Finally, Barnabas insists that John Mark, who abandoned him and Paul on their first missionary voyage, should be included in their next voyage. For Barnabas, initial failure does not disqualify Mark from the call to discipleship, and we will explore the implications of Barnabas' example for our ministry in chapter 5. Each of these incidents demonstrates how Barnabas uses his gift of encouragement to help others understand and follow their own call from Christ.

Encouragement as Ministry

The ministry of encouragement is the art of leading and supporting others in the discovery of their own spiritual gifts and call to discipleship. While some people have the spiritual gift of encouragement to an extraordinary degree, I believe encouragement is a gift all of us in the shared ministry of the church must take seriously. We are all capable of developing this gift, and we are all called to do so. We can "become" a Barnabas. Encouragement is a vital gift for pastors, for it is through this spiritual gift and discipline that we will help congregations discover their own gifts and mission and, I believe, come to a clearer understanding of our gifts and mission as pastors. This is not to say that encouragement is a gift that comes only to the ordained. Longtime leaders within the congregation often are "longtime" precisely because they have this gift and make use of it. Obviously, length of service is not always a guarantee of effective leadership, so wise pastors and lay leaders will make it a priority to discover which laypeople within the congregation are gifted encouragers and challenge them to develop their gift. Whether the process is initiated by pastors or within the lay leadership, the development of a core of "encouragers" within the congregation not only adds to the leadership pool but also generates more creativity and sense of shared commitment to the ministries of the church. Chapter 2 looks at shared ministry in more detail.

While encouragement is important on an individual level, it is even more so for the congregation as a community. As we shall see, the ministry of encouragement is the primary way the pastor and lay leaders help a congregation discover and fulfill its call from Christ to make disciples. One of the advantages of evaluating ministry through the lens of encouragement is that any congregation, regardless of size, location, or level of self-understanding, can benefit. Encouragement allows the congregation to shape its ministry around its strengths rather than to base its work on some model derived from another congregation's story, another pastor's experience. It avoids the one-size-fits-all tyranny of the successful that blinds too many of us to the real strengths and opportunities for ministry available to us in the congregations we serve. Ministry is just as real in the trenches of Nineveh as it is in glamorous Tarshish, and ministry in Tarshish requires the same building of foundations as it does in Nineveh.

Encouragement as Shared Leadership

The ministry of encouragement moves the pastor or pastoral staff out of the center of a church's ministry. More accurately, it makes room for lay leaders to join the pastor and staff in the center and to share their power, responsibility, gifts, and insight. Too often, both pastor and congregation act as though the church's power supply is limited. This misconception can result in a struggle for control within the congregation or between congregation and pastor rather than in a true partnership in ministry. The most common results of this struggle are the attitude that the pastor should design and oversee the church's ministry, or the reverse, that the pastor cannot be trusted to do what is best for the congregation and must have limited influence over the church's ministry. In either case, power and responsibility for ministry are limited to a clique that can manage the power; that is, keep it "where it belongs."

Both of these attitudes ignore the reality that our power source for ministry is the Holy Spirit. By the very nature of the Spirit, the church's power for ministry is unlimited. A group of 120 people gathered in a single place was empowered to reach 3,000 new converts on Pentecost and to continue to grow throughout a sometimes indifferent, often hostile empire. Two uneducated fishermen from Galilee healed a lame man and faced down the leaders of the Temple with holy boldness. In the parish I serve, members of a Disciple Bible Study group[3] became convinced that it was time for the community food pantry to make clothing as well as food available to pantry users. Of course, adding clothing to food as a service meant that more space would be needed. Space requirements led the pantry organizers to join the leaders of the church-sponsored tutoring program in leasing a building that could house a village community center. At the time the lease was signed, the center had no budget and no income, but community businesses and other village churches caught the dream and came to the center's support. Just three months later, the rent and utilities expenses for the remainder of the year were covered. Besides the food pantry, clothing center, and tutoring program, the center now hosts Alcoholics Anonymous, a prayer room, a Sunday evening Bible study, a diabetic support group, a dance exercise class, and an exercise class for seniors. We have been approached by a licensed social worker to begin a program for "at-risk" children through the school system. Although this process of growth has not been without problems or conflicts, the ministry has outstripped what even the most optimistic of us thought possible.

When we think about the events of that first Pentecost, we often emphasize the 3,000 new Christians gained that morning—drawn to the scene by the extraordinary gift of languages given to the followers of Jesus that day and converted by Peter's teaching and preaching. As we see later in the chapter (Acts 2:42-47), the church continued to grow; however, through less spectacular but no less Spirit-filled gifts—the daily worship, work, and care of the community. Although apostles were clearly leaders of this community, every individual was responsible for ministry. Luke shows us in the story of the calling of deacons (Acts 6:1-6) that ministry was initiated according to the needs perceived within the church community. The apostles recognized that the need brought to them was genuine but did not "fix" the problem. Instead, they challenged those who had perceived the need and its cause to find and put the solution into effect. Insight, gifts, responsibility, and power were all shared in the process of resolving the problem; a possible source of division became an opportunity for ministry. Drawing upon the gifts, ordinary and extraordinary, given by God, and upon the guidance of the Spirit, the church of Acts invited every individual to share in the church's work. Although the message that drew people to the church was the promise of salvation, it was the daily living out of new life in community that demonstrated the reality of the promise. As we shall see, ministry in the early church was guided by the Spirit, but ministry was embraced by the whole community.

In too many congregations today, we talk about the limitations and blocks to ministry and allow our ministry to be defined—and therefore limited—by the difficulties that face it. As Luke demonstrates over and over (in the days immediately after Pentecost, in Antioch, in the Council of Jerusalem) the church of Acts operated on a different set of assumptions—assumptions that could guide our congregations equally well. The more ministry we do, the more power we receive; the more faithful we are in discipleship, the more ministry we create; and the more we accept the Spirit's guidance, the less any one person or clique can be or will want to be in control. As we shall see, the ministry of encouragement is grounded in the assumption that these principles are no less true for us than they were for the church of Acts.[4]

Qualities of the Encouraging Leader

Encouragement is not mere cheerleading, nor does it release us from the need to speak truthfully. In fact, the ministry of encouragement will invariably lead to confrontation and difficulty. The ministry of encouragement leads to growth, not to preservation of the status quo. As the effects of encouragement alter a congregation's ministry, some will resist the change we face in all areas of life. As I have shown above, encouragement seeks to broaden the church's base of leadership and to include those whose gifts and ideas have been left on the sidelines. But the ministry of encouragement requires more than sharing leadership to be effective. Succeeding chapters look at these issues in greater detail, but a brief word about them here might be helpful.

Humility

Encouragement demands that we lead out of a true sense of humility, the knowledge of both our gifts and our limitations. Humility is not a false modesty that pretends we do not know our own gifts or that those gifts are not valuable. Neither is humility a method for avoiding responsibility by insisting that someone else would be better equipped to lead or a more appropriate choice for leadership, when such is not the case. On the other hand, humility keeps us from overvaluing our gifts, from being "puffed up." It helps us avoid the traps of conceit and arrogance. In contrast to false modesty and arrogance, humility requires that we accept our gifts and develop them as fully as we can, given our limitations. Humility calls us to make the best use of what has God has given us. An important value of humility for the ministry of encouragement is that it gives us empathy for the struggle others have in discerning the gifts and calling God has given them; humility makes our encouragement authentic. In seeking support for his ministry in Antioch and standing aside for Paul in Cyprus, Barnabas became an example of humility.

The Ability to Deal with Conflict

Encouragement will require us to accept and deal creatively with conflict. A common theme throughout this book is that encouragement will introduce a new way of doing things for many pastors and congregations. We all know that change or the possibility of change is often threatening to people, ourselves included. But we also see in Acts that conflict brings opportunity for insight and growth. The creation of deacons, the Council of Jerusalem, the disagreement between Paul and Barnabas over the role of John Mark—all these led to enhanced ministry. If we follow a ministry of encouraging others to discover their own gifts and ministries, rather than continuing pre-existing programs and committees, we can expect the resistance and criticism that normally accompanies change. Some congregational leaders and members may not only refuse to cooperate but also resist the more enthusiastic, rejecting the new possibilities offered by shared ministry. Pastors and lay leaders alike may have to deal with their own discomfort when the path takes an unexpected turn or when our hopes and expectations are derailed by the surprising winds of the Spirit. The primary example of conflict and creative response in Acts is the discomfort and resistance of many Jewish Christians to the acceptance of Gentiles into Christ's family and the defense of this acceptance by Peter, Paul, Barnabas, and the Council of Jerusalem.

Vulnerability

Because encouragement involves conflict, it requires acceptance of vulnerability on several levels. As we have already noted, discerning and implementing ministry through the process of encouragement will conflict with the image of leadership many people have. While this dilemma is particularly acute for pastors, who often have well-defined traditional roles and expectations within a given congregation, it will also affect lay leaders. (In fact, it can be a most difficult source of conflict when the lay leadership accepts and works well with ministry by encouragement but the pastor is not yet on board.) Ministry by encouragement takes seriously the ministry of all believers and tries to expand the circle of ministers beyond the select few. Encouragement will sometimes require saying no where we once said yes—no to attending and controlling the agenda for every meeting, no to the idea that ministry should never fail or make mistakes, no to the idea that ministry should be conflict-free, no to the idea that the pastor or other leaders should always get their way. All these nos will violate a lot of comfort zones, including our own, and make us vulnerable to criticism and resistance. Yet effective ministry requires us to accept this vulnerability. Effective ministry will also require us to be honest about our own limitations, fears, and struggles, not indiscriminately or in a manipulative manner, but with an honest and supportive group of colleagues. Scripture is full of vulnerable leaders, not just Barnabas. Jesus himself, particularly in his dealings with the obtuseness of the disciples and the false expectations of the crowd, showed the necessity of vulnerability. We also see vulnerability in the painful passages of Paul's letters, Jeremiah's complaints, and the psalms of lament.

Integrity

Encouragement requires that we lead from integrity, for if we are leading by trust in prayer and the Spirit, we must both trust and be trustworthy. It should go without saying that encouragement should not be embraced on the surface, only to be undercut behind the scenes. If we are going to follow the Spirit, we must genuinely let go of control. Ananias, Sapphira, and Simon Magus all demonstrate the danger of trying to manipulate the Spirit for our own ends. At the same time, stepping back from control does not equal stepping away from work. If anything, encouragement requires more communication, more prayer and study, more listening and dreaming together than leadership by a CEO or an inner circle. The quality of integrity demanded by encouragement requires faith in the Spirit, faith in oneself, and the creation of a method for accountability to Christ and to each other. The Council of Jerusalem again, the break between Barnabas and Paul over John Mark's reliability and potential, and Peter's struggles with the "Gentile question" all illustrate the importance of integrity to our shared ministry.

All of these requirements—sharing power and responsibility, humility, dealing creatively with conflict, vulnerability, integrity—will appear and reappear in the discussion that follows. They are interrelated—it is impossible to say where humility stops and integrity begins or exactly how the ability or inability to share power and responsibility affects how well or badly we deal with conflict. Issues will rise around these qualities, their existence or absence, throughout our ministry, and that reality is reflected in the chapters that follow. The ministry of encouragement gives us one effective way to understand these qualities and to make them a positive presence in ministry.

TWO

Standing With and Standing Aside

The Ministry of Partnership

Barnabas then left for Tarsus to look for Saul, and when he found him he brought him to Antioch. And it happened that they stayed together in that church a whole year, instructing a large number of people. It was at Antioch that the disciples were first called "Christians."—Acts 11:25-26

THESE WORDS FROM ACTS RELATE the sequel to Barnabas' evaluation trip to Antioch. He has been sent to Antioch by the home church in Jerusalem to appraise and support the mission begun by his fellow Cypriot Christians. He finds a congregation that is part Jewish and part Gentile but united in Christ and vibrant with the Spirit. The question arises: Where does this church go from here? For the first time, large numbers of people outside Jerusalem have been converted and have joined the church. How are they to be nurtured in the faith? The task is complicated by the diversity of the members. Some have been brought up in the familiar faith of Abraham, Isaac, Jacob, and Moses, the faith of Jesus and the disciples. But many more have not. How are

11

they to be taught this faith with its rich heritage? How can they be helped to understand the covenants between God and his people that underpin their new faith?

This process of instruction and maturation in the Christian faith is often called "sanctification." Sanctification is a necessary part of growth in faith, the ongoing process of keeping faith a vital part of one's life. Philip's encounter with the Ethiopian official in Acts 8 and Peter's with the household of Cornelius in Acts 10 raise the question of how to bring Gentiles into this process of sanctification, but it is in Antioch that the question is raised on a large scale. How does spiritual growth take place within a diverse congregation? This is the task that Barnabas has inherited as Jerusalem's representative to the new church.

Barnabas responds to his assignment with appropriate humility. He is aware of his own gifts and talents, but he is also aware of his limitations. Perhaps he is overwhelmed by the sheer numbers of people needing instruction and support; perhaps he mistrusts his abilities as teacher or simply believes that the situation calls for someone who can complement his gifts. Whatever his reasoning, Barnabas makes the trip from Antioch to Tarsus to recruit a partner whose abilities and energy he has come to know and trust. The relationship between Saul and Barnabas began with Barnabas serving as Saul's sponsor. It now becomes a partnership in ministry that will change the scope and face of Christianity.

Luke does not tell us the methodology or content of Barnabas' and Saul's work. He merely tells us that the pair "instruct[ed] a large number of people." Their instruction was sufficiently distinctive and effective that the people of the new congregation became known as Christians. In other words, the unique message of Christ that Barnabas and Saul communicated led Christ's followers in Antioch to act in a distinctively "Christian" way. Whether we understand the pair's efforts as

Christian education, preaching, spiritual direction, or a mixture of all three, it was powerful and transformational. The congregation in Antioch continued to grow and continued to develop an identity distinct from Judaism and other local religions.

As Acts 13:1-5 demonstrates, the mission impulse in Antioch soon grew beyond providing fellowship and relief for other followers of Christ, support shown in Acts 11:27-30 (Antioch's collection of funds for the home church in Jerusalem). Up to this point, spreading the Word seems to have been a matter of individual opportunity and response. In Antioch, the urge to share the good news resulted in a call to a new direction for ministry. As the leaders of the congregation gathered in worship and prayer, the Spirit spoke to them, designating Barnabas and Saul as servants to be set apart for a special mission. Luke's account is not clear as to whether this was a regular time of worship or whether the leaders were seeking special guidance from the Holy Spirit. Possibly this ambiguity reflects the fact that the ancient church, less inclined than we to separate worship from "church work," always gathered in awareness of the Spirit's presence and the need for the Spirit's guidance. In any case, after a period of preparation involving fasting and prayer, the two were commissioned with the laying on of hands and sent on the first missionary journey. In these verses, we are shown for the first time how the process of congregational discernment can work, and we see that the partnership in ministry demonstrated by Barnabas and Saul can also be effective on a congregational level.

Notice this process of discerning and calling. First, the congregational leaders prepare themselves for the guidance of the Spirit through *shared worship and prayer*. This practice is very different from that of many contemporary church meetings, whose emphasis is often on getting to the business as quickly as possible after, at most, a brief devotion. The next step is to *seek the Spirit's guidance*. The assumption in Antioch was that the agenda, goals, and actions needed for ministry come directly from Christ through the agency of the Spirit. Once the goal (sharing the gospel beyond Antioch) and action (sending Barnabas and Saul to preach in Cyprus) are established, a present-day congregation might move directly to get the mission underway. In Antioch, a third and fourth step intervene. Ministry is preceded by a time of *spiritual preparation, specifically prayer and fasting.* This preparation is not limited to Barnabas and Saul; the whole leadership and possibly the entire congregation participate. Even then, Barnabas and Saul are not sent off to Cyprus as lone rangers. Barnabas and Saul are *empowered as representatives of Christ and the congregation* of Antioch through the laying on of hands. Their commission comes from the community through the Spirit.

Every step of this ministry is a partnership between the congregation at Antioch, those chosen for mission, and the Holy Spirit. The guidance of the Spirit is not merely hoped for, nor is it an abstraction. By making prayer a vital part of each step, the congregation at Antioch allowed the Spirit to shape its ministry. Once the goal and action were discerned, the church followed the pattern for mission established by Jesus; the missionaries are sent out as a pair, not as solitary individuals, and they begin ministry by forming local partnerships in the places they are sent. Ministry is not individual and is not begun without the nourishment provided by communal prayer and fasting. The norm for New Testament ministry is partnership—even Philip's apparently solitary encounter with the Ethiopian official is initiated by the Spirit's intervention (Acts 8:26).

Encouragement as Partnership

How does this process work in a contemporary congregation? Following the general outline offered in Acts 13, we have tried a new way of approaching ministry at First United Methodist in Mount Sterling. As the congregational leaders did in Antioch, we began with prayer. The initial prayers were my own, as I asked for help in listening to church members and other people from the community speak of their needs and dreams. During this period of prayer, I asked for help in discerning who might help discover a new vision for the church. Through prayer and the conversations I was led to have through prayer, it quickly became clear that a hunger for spiritual growth was present in the congregation and that many gifted laypeople felt that their gifts were not fully used. A number of people told me that they had no real idea of how to pray beyond their own morning devotions. They had never been a part of corporate prayer, other than the prayers of the liturgy or mealtime grace; and they did not understand its potential. Others felt no real connection between their lives and Scripture and had no idea how to discover that connection. The problem of underused members was related to the way ministry was planned and supported at First Church. Instead of drawing upon the wide variety of gifts and experiences within the whole congregation, our leadership pool consisted of 10 or 12 people who always seemed to end up with the responsibility of seeing that the ministry was done. This situation often left those outside the pool with the impression that their gifts were neither necessary nor valuable to the church.

The next step was a natural outgrowth of my own prayer—inviting the congregation to join me. All church members were invited to become involved in prayer groups and studies about prayer, but I drew upon the model of Antioch and specifically approached a dozen people to become prayer partners with me. Some of these were men and women whose names had come to me in prayer; others had shared their interest in the church's ministry. This group consisted of a mixture of church leaders and those who had felt left out of the leadership loop. We made a commitment to pray daily for the ministry of the congregation. This dozen took the initiative to invite others, so that in less than a month I was surprised to discover that nearly 30 men and women out of a congregation of 250 were involved in prayer for the church and for new growth in ministry. This was just the first point at which the congregation moved faster and more effectively than I expected.

During this first year of communal prayer and listening, I preached through the book of Acts and encouraged people to ask how the church's current ministry—both the programs that were active and the way we carried them out—paralleled the ministry of the apostles' church and how it did not. In conversations and meetings, I listened for those who wanted to see First Church extend its ministry to the community, for those who were dreaming of new possibilities, even for those who were dissatisfied but could not express a solid reason for their discontent. Some were already leaders in the church; some were attending but otherwise inactive. We began an informal series of gatherings at the parsonage on Sunday afternoons at which people shared their hopes for the church. We prayed for guidance: How might we make these hopes come to reality? Were our hopes in tune with God's intent for us?

What emerged from these meetings was a sense that business as usual—with the committees we had in place and the ways we tried to do ministry—was simply not bearing sufficient fruit. As I have said, the leadership pool consisted of about a dozen in a church of 250 members. Because both the ideas for ministry and the people entrusted to carry them out came from this small pool, the meetings tended to focus on the difficulties and impossibilities of ministry rather than on possibilities. The idea of stepping out in faith that God would provide for ministry sounded like a foreign language. Much meeting time was spent lamenting the lack of participation by the larger congregation, but when names of possible participants were brought forward, the leaders were reluctant to approach them:

"Well, he's busy, too."

"She has children to look after."

(I hasten to say that I do not believe this reaction was a deliberate exclusion of others. Rather, our leaders felt that asking others to participate was an intrusion, not the offering of an opportunity.) A significant portion of the ministry that was under way had been started because someone outside the committee structure just went ahead and did it. In the exploration meetings we held at the parsonage, people shared their conviction that they, and others, did want to do more but lacked a sense of direction. A significant number felt that recent pastors had neither helped the leadership express a vision for ministry nor helped develop new leadership. Little sense of partnership prevailed, either with the Spirit or between pastor and laity.

Nearly a year after the initial prayer group began and in a moment that was truly Spirit-led, our administrative board and I decided to take a one-year vacation from all standing committees other than those required for church business by the *United Methodist Book of Discipline.* Instead, we would substitute a council on lay ministries that would be responsible for helping laypeople carry out the ministries to which they were called. We expanded the number of potential partners in ministry by inviting anyone to participate who had an idea for new ministry or simply an interest in the ministry of the church, but we also drew a core group from those who had come to the parsonage "dreaming sessions" to help get the council off the ground. No idea would be discouraged; we would ask not "Can we do this?" but "How can we help this happen?"

I have to admit that special grace was with us in this process. My only contact with such a council had been the prior fall. I had been invited to a nearby United Methodist church to make a presentation about AIDS ministry to its lay council, and what I saw in that meeting led me to believe that a similar council might suit our search for a new way of planning and recruiting. I had not read any of the materials available on this type of council and had not really thought through how the process might work. While the council on lay ministries has worked well for us, we probably spent more time spinning our wheels around questions of membership (did we really have a policy that meetings were open to all interested members, or did participation need to be by election?) and procedure (did we use consensus or *Robert's Rules of Order* or some hybrid?) than we might have spent had we drawn upon an existing model. We didn't even contact the church where I had attended the council meeting—another bit of grace, as it happened, for its leaders had given up on the idea a few months after my visit. They had found it too difficult to persuade their members to depart from the more traditional United Methodist structure.

Two factors may have helped the council work in our setting. First was the positive response we drew by eliminating the lag between planning a ministry and beginning it. We no longer had to get the proper committee's approval, refer it to our administrative board for its approval, and then send it back to the committee to complete whatever recruiting, funding, and training might be needed to begin the ministry. Moving from meeting to meeting could sometimes add two to three months between idea and execution and effectively eliminate the enthusiasm of those who had originated the idea.

The other aid to acceptance: those who had an idea for ministry took the lead on planning; the council's role as ministry partner was to offer support, to help with recruitment and publicity, to evaluate the results, to offer suggestions, and otherwise help the ministry develop. While such an outcome was possible under the previous structure, in practice the standing committees did not do well at hearing ideas other than their own or helping people not part of the committees develop their own ideas and calls to ministry.

At this point we decided to use Acts 13 as our model. The first step was to allow the Spirit to lead our agenda. This does not mean we sat in passive silence. We assumed that the Spirit reaches us through our discussion of the perceived needs of the community and congregation, through attention to the gifts needed to meet those needs, and through the experience and imagination of the members in attendance. But we took seriously the first step in the process and began each meeting with prayer for guidance. If we reached a sticky point in our discussion, we prayed again, asking for clarity. Our working assumption was that if someone had an idea for ministry, the idea came from the Spirit. Our role was to work in partnership with the Spirit and each other to help that ministry become effective, as the church at Antioch supported the mission to Cyprus. Once we accepted an idea for a new ministry, we then agreed as a council to become prayer partners for the guidance and protection of the ministries and for those carrying it out, the third step in the process. When necessary, we put into place a temporary support committee to help the ministry get off the ground and to evaluate its effectiveness. Finally, we recognized those leading or participating in the ministry through announcements, newsletter articles, and a yearly celebration of volunteers in the ministries of the church.

We were perhaps naïve, but we did not worry much about whether the ministries presented to us truly came from the Spirit. Certainly, both Satan and our own sinful nature can lead us astray in ministry, but we felt that we were protected by the power of our collective prayer and by the conversations we shared during the council meetings. Only once did I feel that we might be doing a ministry for the wrong reason: we chose to try an outreach program for children patterned on one already successful in another local church. My own feeling was that we were possibly pursuing the program out of chagrin that another congregation had it and we did not. I foolishly kept my reservations to myself, worried that I might exert too much influence over the discussion. When we tried the program, it expired within two months from a lack of volunteers. We returned to prayer and discussion and developed a different ministry that filled a need rather than duplicating another church's success. Plenty of volunteers emerged for this ministry.

In other cases, if the ministry did not work well at first try, we assumed a need to listen to the Spirit again, possibly rethinking the process for carrying out that ministry or changing its focus. For instance, our plans for shepherding individuals and families who began attending First Church—connecting visitors with companions and information to help integrate them into the congregation—hit a snag early on. We discovered that we had not allowed for visiting patterns or for differences in people's comfort level. We might experience six weeks with no new visitors, during which time our shepherds would wonder when they might get to use their training. Then we might have eight visitors at a time when only a couple of shepherding families were available. We discovered also that some people felt welcomed by immediate personal contact and invitation and some felt smothered. So we rethought our approach—now the first contact with visitors is by a lay member of the church, who usually telephones or sends a card. Then, if visitors show enough interest to return, a family or couple from the church initiates a more personal contact and stays in touch at the visitor's or prospective member's comfort level. If the visitors have a prior relationship with the church (for example, through the food pantry or day-care program), we move directly to a personal contact. We also have enlarged the pool of shepherds to include more recent members of the church, not just longtime members.

At times, a ministry suggestion emerged from our prayer and discussion that was inappropriate or not well thought out. Usually when this happened, the person who brought the original idea to the council recognized the problem as we talked and either withdrew it or accepted insights that helped it grow into a new and better possibility. An example of such an outcome was an idea for reaching out to the growing Mexican immigrant population in our community—a proposal that failed to consider both the language barrier and the Roman Catholic origins of most of the new arrivals. After we talked through the difficulties we might encounter without sensitivity to both these realities, we decided to begin with a basic service, offering classes in English as a second language (ESL) to those who desired them, and allowing other ministries to grow from what we learned in the relationships between the tutors and students.

As I noted, this has not been a tidy process, and communication within the council and congregation needs as much attention as, if not more than, under the old system. When the prior committees were in place, the area of responsibility and contact person were usually clearly defined. Now we have to be certain that a person is assigned to handle communications for a ministry and that accountability is established between the council and the ministry team. Partners need to pay as much attention to lines of communication as committees do. Still, our ministry has expanded, and the list of people active in ministry has grown.

Even old stand-bys such as vacation Bible school and recruitment of church-school teachers are now organized through this process, beginning with prayer that the Spirit will help us carry out the ministry. When our church-school superintendent resigned, we did not begin flinging out the names of possible

replacements or start phoning prospects. Instead we prayed together and simply advertised the need in the announcements
before worship. It took only two weeks before Pat stepped forward to volunteer for the position. Although fall classes were
only a month away, we decided to try the same approach to fill
the teaching slots that remained. Two Sundays later (rather than
the normal six- to eight-week process of phoning potential teachers), these positions were also filled; four people volunteered
who had never previously taught. Those who chose to share
their motivation for volunteering spoke of the congregation's
prayers. They knew from hearing those prayers that teachers
were a concern for the church, and they felt a nudge or a call to
offer their time and gifts.

Could this have happened under the old committee system? Perhaps. But during this period of change, we reminded
ourselves what had been forgotten under that system—that all
members should consider themselves partners in ministry, not
just those serving on committees. Our constant attention to
prayer, particularly to prayer as ministry, spoke to the congregational hunger for more spiritual depth in our life together. Standing committees have their uses, and we are beginning to
re-establish them in areas where our ministry is well defined
and ongoing. The biggest differences between our present committees and their predecessors are the explicit attention we now
pay to the Spirit's guidance and the effort we make to involve
people other than committee members in a ministry. Keeping
these partnerships alive requires constant attention from us all.

After two years of prayer and nearly 18 months after adopt-
ing our Spirit-led approach, First Church had begun a tutoring
program in the village elementary school, reopened and staffed
our Sunday-morning nursery, cosponsored two ecumenical healing ministry weekends with the Deer Creek Cooperative Ministry (of which we are a member), purchased a church van, begun

a young-adult ministry group, expanded our prayer ministry team, involved nearly 10 percent of the congregation in Disciple Bible Study, formed a worship team to evaluate how to involve more laity in worship and when and how to begin a new worship service, and initiated a long-hoped-for community center. While I lent support to all of these, I initiated none of them. I did not and do not meet with any of the support committees, other than the worship team, except by invitation. Rather, these ministries were developed through the imagination and commitment of individual lay members and the council for lay ministries after a process of prayer and attentiveness to the Spirit. Although by general principle we invite the council and congregation to pray over a potential ministry for a time before committing to it, new ministries are actually begun more quickly than under the old committee and board system.

Our "one-year experiment" has entered its third year. We do find that we need some committee work outside the council meeting, but these committees are generally driven by a single task and continue past their expected time of service only with the consent of both council and committee. The expected time is usually event driven—the time it takes to plan and carry out a vacation Bible school—or until a ministry takes on a life that requires more attention than one or two people can provide. We have established three standing committees so far: evangelism, children's ministries, and prayer ministries. These are in addition to the administrative committees needed for the operation of the church—personnel, trustees, and stewardship. Ministries that need less formal planning stay under the supervision of those who brought them to the council. One example would be our "care bag" ministry: two volunteers make up bags of snacks, an appropriate card, and personalized games or puzzles for people in the hospital or temporarily unable to get around. Another group provides dinners for families who have suffered loss. When members or funds are needed or when someone is ready to step out of this particular ministry, the group returns to the council to ask for help. The council either provides people and resources or brings the need to prayer.

This transition has not been without problems. We will take a closer look at some of these in the final chapter, but a couple of tensions that have surfaced throughout merit mention here. Some resistance has arisen, particularly among church members who feel displaced by this process. Two members (I'll call them Joan and Harry) who had served in leadership for several terms and on a variety of committees did not respond to invitations to be a part of any of the prayer groups, studies, or parsonage meetings. Consequently, neither received a personal invitation to be a part of the council on lay ministries, although they were included in the general invitation to all members. Neither Harry nor Joan expressed disappointment to me directly, but they voiced some frustration and hurt to other members that they had not received a special invitation. When I paid each a visit to explain, each accepted my explanation, but some coolness remained toward the council and me. The next fall, as we made nominations for our administrative committees, each was asked to accept a position. Harry accepted and serves on our staff-parish (personnel) committee. Joan has chosen not to participate on committees or boards of the church. Both continue to express doubts about the new direction, although both support the ministries themselves.

Other tensions persist. Some members simply continue to assume that the pastor is responsible for all ministry decisions, regardless of what they are told by other laity. Joan's situation is not unique. Others share doubts about the process and are critical of it. Some critics are willing to share those doubts with me; others do not come to me directly. I am sometimes frustrated by their unwillingness to talk openly about their concerns, but I believe that the best I can do is to trust the lay leaders, to trust that the Spirit is leading us as we need to go, and to continue being the best pastor I can be to all members. Fortunately, disagreements about the process of ministry have not, for the most part, eroded pastoral or personal relationships among us.

Overall, reliance on the Spirit and on partnership among the pastor and church members has changed how we do ministry for the better. I believe that our growth in membership, while modest by megachurch standards, is a sign that others in the community are sensing and responding to the Spirit's presence. This may not be a model that will work in all churches in every detail; larger churches may need to adapt to a larger leadership group and to the presence and varied needs of the several communities contained within the larger group. Still, I firmly believe that the four-step process described in Acts 13 will have a positive effect on ministry in any congregation that follows it faithfully.

The Encouraging Pastor as Partner

We have been living for some time, at least in Protestant America, with the limitations of pastor-driven programming and leadership by professionals. We have been sold the idea that ordained pastors or professionally trained laity are the only leaders who have the expertise to develop and evaluate the programs of the church. The weaknesses of top-down leadership have been recognized within the business world for some time, and processes have been developed to meet these weaknesses. In the church, though, we too often pay lip service to the importance of the ministry of the laity while continuing to expect that the really important and effective ideas will come from the offices and studies of pastors and denominational officials. This assumption can lead to a "let the pastor do it" mind-set, creating unrealistic expectations for the pastor's leadership, undervaluing the ideas and capabilities of laity, and leading to clergy burnout and lay apathy.

Certainly, pastors have an important role to play in developing the ministry of a congregation. But the pastor's traditional roles of preaching, teaching, and pastoral care have often been swallowed up by the relatively recent notion that the pastor should oversee the ministry of the whole congregation, becoming involved at every level of planning and execution. Many pastors complain of a sense of spiritual dryness, dissatisfaction, and disconnectedness. Such feelings can derive from the sense that we are investing spiritual and physical energy toward a call that is not our own. It is hard to imagine John Wesley or Martin Luther or John Knox accepting the schedules of their ordained descendants and dedicating two to three nights a week to attending board and committee meetings. I earlier referred to Acts 6:1-6 as an example of developing ministry in response to congregational and community needs. This passage also demonstrates that clergy should not accept tasks that pull them away from their proper role. The issue was not that the problem (giving equal attention to the needs of all widows within the church) was unimportant or beneath the apostles. The point was that others could attend to the solution while the apostles remained centered on their proper task: "[We] will give our attention to prayer and the ministry of the word" (Acts 6:6). Ordained pastors are called to a ministry of preaching, teaching, and the care of souls. Too often, we are expected by our congregations, pastoral supervisors, and ourselves to fulfill roles and administer tasks that could easily—and often more competently—be done by laypeople.[1]

In his study *Stress, Power, and Ministry* Jack Harris looks at, among a host of helpful insights, the conflict created by false images of the pastor's role—both self-imposed images and those projected by the congregation. When the pastor is expected—by himself or herself or by laity—to be a hero without flaw or to act as autocratic CEO, the ministry of the laity is wounded and the pastor will be unable to fulfill conflicting expectations. While Harris uses the term "collaboration" rather than "partnership," the implication for ministry is the same: "shared power between pastor and people . . . in the development of the local church's ministry." Harris continues:

> From this perspective, the pastor is seen, not as *the* sacramental person, but as one sacramental presence among many in a rich, differentiated expression of functions, talents, individuals and tasks in the congregation's life. Pastors are learning to see that having influence does not mean calling all the shots.

Harris identifies the capacity for autonomy as essential to the pastor's role:

> a capacity to balance and resolve opposing demands within themselves and between them and their congregations. . . . [S]uch a capacity does not imply power *over* the members but power *with* them. It does not contradict the concept of ministry as servanthood but is its essential ingredient.[2]

As I note below, my becoming partner rather than CEO has not only allowed new leaders to develop within the congregation; it has also allowed me to develop new aspects of my own ministry.

Encouragement as Standing Aside

As we follow this process of Spirit-led ministry, we eventually will be surprised to discover that we, pastors and laity alike, have lost control of the direction our ministry takes. This situation is not a bad thing. Well-controlled ministries are often stagnant ministries that meet our goals, not necessarily God's. But

Spirit-led ministry does call for a certain muting of ego. This struggle between the human need for control and the call to give up ourselves for Christ has been recognized and experienced by church leaders of every age. Traditionally, the Methodist societies established by John Wesley and the churches of the Wesleyan tradition have affirmed the need to commit and recommit to following Christ in a service held to observe the New Year. At the heart of this Covenant Service is a prayer of commitment that says in one phrase, "Let me be employed by Thee or let me be laid aside for Thee."[3] The second clause can be harder to accept than the first. Again, Barnabas can give us insight into the power of standing aside.

As Barnabas and Saul began their ministry on Cyprus, an apparently minor encounter changed the shape of their partnership. As they preached the gospel to the proconsul of Cyprus, one of his attendants, a magician named Elymas, attempted to interfere "so as to prevent the proconsul's conversion to the faith" (Acts 13:8). Saul confronted the magician and by his words temporarily blinded him. The proconsul, suitably impressed, became a believer. What is most significant for us in this confrontation is that Saul for the first time took precedence in the partnership. From this point on, Luke refers to Barnabas and Saul as "Paul and Barnabas," or even as "Paul and his companions." Although this seems a small detail, Luke is well known by scholars for his careful craftsmanship, and the change in order would seem a deliberate choice by the author. The change in order signifies a change in role; Paul has become senior partner over his former sponsor. Luke is characteristically light on details we would be fascinated to hear. Is this shift by prior agreement? Does it occur because Paul is a better preacher or more charismatic? Or it is a function of Barnabas' ministry as encourager that he naturally recedes into the background as his partner gains assurance? Luke leaves us to speculate, but the change in position is clear.[4]

For Paul to use his gifts fully and to fulfill his ministry, Barnabas had to give up his position as leader of their mission and allow Paul to follow the Spirit's leading. It is not too much to say that the Spirit's call to Barnabas *at this point* was to be "laid aside" for Christ and to accept Paul's leadership. One of the hardest lessons for leaders to learn is how to relinquish control of ministry to allow others to fulfill their call. This is true for pastoral and lay leaders alike, though lay leaders rarely carry the role expectations described in the previous section. Still, relinquishing control is a natural and necessary part of Christian ministry. Sometimes being "laid aside" occurs when we are affected by illness or personal crisis, sometimes when we reach retirement age or, in the case of clergy, when we are asked to leave a particular congregation. Clergy are not the only ones reluctant to accept such occasions. We all remember the teacher, musician, or treasurer who could no longer perform the required duties well but resisted being "put out to pasture." We all know people who find it difficult to let go of responsibility when their term of office is completed and a successor is named. But these examples of being laid aside are not really voluntary—they come through circumstance. When another individual is called to a ministry that is currently my responsibility, it may be necessary for me to *choose* to be "laid aside."

As we have seen, clergy are often handed (and often seek) responsibilities that are not truly their own. They often are given an authority over the ministry of the church that limits the ideas and participation of others. If all Christ's ministers, clergy and lay, are going to use fully the gifts of the Spirit and to fulfill their individual ministries, clergy must be "laid aside" from control of ministry so that the Spirit may call and be heard by all. What Harris calls "collaboration" might also be understood as what Paul calls "putting on the mind of Christ" and "taking on the very nature of a servant" (Phil. 2:5, 7). Relinquishing a position of control to allow someone else to fulfill his or her ministry is the act of a true leader and may indeed add to the pastor's or other leader's legitimate authority within the congregation.

Does this mean that the pendulum swings to the other extreme? Does it mean that I, as pastor, must become a bystander in the church's ministry, as many laity feel they are required to do now? Hardly. Partnership is still a requirement. Helping a congregation prepare to receive the Spirit's guidance is difficult work, not least because many of us, pastors and laity alike, have little training in prayer and little understanding or expectation of the Spirit's real power.[5] The partnership of listening to one another and spending time together in prayer is vital, but it almost certainly will not happen in most congregations without commitment and leadership from the pastor, nor will it continue unless both pastor and lay leaders keep it a priority. Being "laid aside" from control of the congregation's ministry will actually free pastors and lay leaders to seek the Spirit's guidance toward ministries that fit their true gifts and to encourage others within the congregation to do the same.

Making room for new ideas and new leaders is a constant challenge to both lay leaders and pastors. Even now that the lay ministry council is functioning at First Church, the temptation is to slip into the same patterns as the committees the council replaced: narrowing our vision to what has already worked, seeing ourselves as the only leaders available, expecting that only those present at the meeting are capable of planning and doing the church's ministry. To avoid falling into these old traps, congregational leaders need to attend to the continued spiritual growth of the whole congregation (sanctification, again) through worship and education and attention to the process of inviting and creating disciples. We then need to recognize that partnership means sharing power and opportunity for ministry as others within the congregation begin to hear and follow the Spirit's call to discipleship.

Many laypeople and pastors will be uncomfortable with these changes; but this discomfort is an unavoidable reality. In many churches, pastors are expected not only to attend meetings but also to take the lead in creating the agenda. In some, pastors are even expected to control the outcome of committee decisions. I have received criticism for "not doing my job" by some at First Church when the trustees make a decision without my presence at the meeting or when the council decides that laity ought to take more responsibility during worship services. Some refuse to believe that I am not continuing to call the shots behind the scenes. Occasionally, members express frustration that meetings have less structure than they would like, or say they feel that I am a weak pastor because I refuse to direct the decisions of the council. Not all these problems can be resolved to everyone's satisfaction. Many times, though, people who allow themselves to be introduced to the process of discernment come to recognize that Spirit-led ministry is not only viable but is working well.

In all honesty, though, the discomfort of the laity is no greater than my own. I find it hard not to volunteer to make recruitment phone calls or to be one of the van drivers. (How dare they manage ministry without me!) I chafe when I am not asked my opinion on every small detail, and I feel rejected when my opinion *is* asked but the council or ministry team decides on a different course of action. It helps only a little when their decision turns out to be correct. Early in my time at First, I insisted that beginning both Disciple I and Disciple II Bible studies would be a mistake, since so few had signed up when Disciple I was previously offered. The council listened politely, decided to do both anyway, and I had to admit my lack of faith when enough people signed up to create three sections of Disciple. In other words, my ego keeps trying to block the Spirit's work, and I am wrestling with it as much this year as when we began this journey.

But Barnabas calls me to the ministry of encouragement, not to the "ministry" of domination. By releasing myself and the congregation from a false sense of control and by trusting the Spirit to provide the needed guidance for us all, I can offer knowledge of resources, sermons that empower and challenge, and a continued call to communal prayer—all without needing to manage the results. I have been "surprised by joy" when a leader emerges from the fringes of the congregation to fill a needed post. I have now experienced the Spirit's "blowing where it will," taking over a meeting, and catching us up in the currents of new and sometimes unexpected ministry. And personal benefits accrue when my ego isn't "acting out." I enjoy the freedom of missing a meeting to attend to a more pressing pastoral need, knowing that my opinion will be considered fairly during my absence. Having become more confident of their own gifts and leadership, the congregation's members have released me for other ministries, including the ministry to children described in the next chapter, and the writing of this book.

Lovett Weems, director of the Lewis Center for Church Leadership at Wesley Theological Seminary in Washington, D.C., writes in *Leadership in the Wesleyan Spirit*:

> The question [of Christian leadership in the church] is not, "Whom will we select for high positions?" That is an important question, but it is not *the* question. The question God is asking us in the church this day is, "How many priests, how many ministers, how many leaders for God are there throughout the church?". . . It is significant how often there is multiple leadership during periods of church renewal and vitality. . . . It is in such times of revisioning and revival that whole generations of different leaders emerge for the church and society. It is in these eras that conventional assumptions about who can lead do not stop this multiple leadership from flowering, unlimited by class, gender, race, and ordained status distinction.[6]

And, I would add, unlimited by a past history of reluctance to change, fear of failure, or inadequate vision within a given congregation. Opening our hearts and minds to the Spirit overcomes even the past. Spirit-led ministry blows where it will, using the resources it will. Our ministry can be limited only by our refusal to follow.

Reflections

1. How has the Spirit been a partner in the ministry to which you have been called?

   - How has the Spirit been a partner in the ministry of your church and congregation?
   - What personal resources and commitments do you need to shift to a Spirit-led ministry?
   - Who are the key people within the congregation who might help with such a shift?

2. How important is the partnership of corporate prayer to the life of your church?

   - How influenced by prayer and worship are your congregation's "business" meetings?
   - What opportunities for growth in prayer have you experienced in the past year?
   - What kinds of opportunities for growth in prayer have been offered to your congregation?

3. What are the expectations the pastor and congregation hold for pastoral attendance and participation in meetings?

   - How much does the pastor shape the agenda and decisions of congregational and committee meetings?

- How willing are you to be set aside—to become a servant—for Christ and the health of your congregation's ministry?
- How comfortable are you accepting disagreement with your opinion and guidance?
- Where and how do you find support in the partnership of ministry?

THREE

Standing with Outsiders and Outcasts

The Ministry of Hospitality

When he got to Jerusalem, [Saul] tried to join the disciples, but they were all afraid of him: they could not believe he was really a disciple. Barnabas, however, took charge of him, introduced him to the apostles, and explained how the Lord had appeared to him and spoken to him on his journey, and how he had preached fearlessly at Damascus in the name of Jesus.—Acts 9:26-27

I CAN IMAGINE THE STRUGGLE SAUL must have experienced as he approached the church in Jerusalem. He certainly knew how much he was feared and distrusted. He had to have known that the community of believers would continue to remember and loathe his past actions toward their brothers and sisters. Still, I believe Saul's need to set things right, his need for forgiveness and acceptance, was strong enough to overcome his hesitation. So when Saul left Damascus under threat of death, he chose to risk a return to Jerusalem. Luke relates the initial reaction of the church to his arrival, and it was much as we would expect. The disciples were afraid of their former persecutor. They did not trust the transformation he claimed to have undergone; they could not believe that his zeal to destroy the Way could become a passion for the gospel. So they refused his efforts at reconciliation. Saul was not welcome in the church.

At this point (Acts 9:27) Barnabas makes his second appearance in Luke's story. He "takes charge" of Saul. Is he already acquainted with Saul's conversion and his efforts on behalf of Christ? Or is it through a risky and unselfish act of hospitality, Saul's change of heart still unproven, that Barnabas first hears of the Damascus Road and Saul's ministry? We don't really know, although the second version would be consistent with Barnabas' character. Whatever the case, Barnabas becomes Saul's advocate, returning with him to the apostles and speaking on his behalf. He tells Saul's story—the vision on the road that changed him from Christ's enemy to Christ's servant, his first efforts in preaching the good news, the resistance he has faced, and the fruit his efforts have borne. When Barnabas has completed his witness, the enemy is now accepted as a brother. Saul is accepted into the fellowship of the Way and encouraged to continue his mission. He preaches in Jerusalem until opposition makes it necessary for him to return to Tarsus.

In chapter 6 we will examine the importance of integrity to the ministry of encouragement, but it is worth noting now the vital role Barnabas' character as a man of integrity plays in this context. Barnabas is convincing as Saul's advocate because the apostles know and respect him. Although he is outside the central core of leadership (the apostles are based in Jerusalem— Barnabas is from Cyprus), he has established a track record that gives him credibility with that core. The church's regard for him is shown even in the new name he has received from them— Barnabas, son of encouragement. Barnabas has invested his property, his time and energy, and his former name in supporting the church and in carrying the good news of Christ. He has evidently impressed his fellows with his ability to evaluate others as well as to encourage them, so when he speaks for Saul, the apostles are willing to accept from him what Saul could not convincingly declare on his own. *Who Barnabas is* matters to his ministry.

The connection between character and effective ministry Barnabas demonstrates may seem self-evident, but clergy often make problems for themselves by not recognizing that personal integrity does matter to their congregations. This lack of recognition can lead to the donning of "masks" by clergy—hiding aspects of their character or personality that they feel might be difficult for congregations to understand or accept. These traits can be minor and range from an earthy sense of humor or a quick temper—each of which can be problematic in the parish—to a love for music and literature that is not overtly Christian or a taste for fine cooking (which may be viewed by congregational members or colleagues as insufficiently spiritual interests for a pastor). Of course, masks can also be used to hide major flaws that carry major consequences: an inability to deal with criticism, a loss of faith, or a need to exert power through sexual liaisons. What clergy often do not recognize is that the construction of masks to hide even a minor dissonance creates a separation between the inner reality of a person and the outer projection, a separation that can easily result in a lack of authenticity. Ironically, this inauthenticity can cause more conflict and harm than dealing with the original problem would. Such a separation between the inner and outer person can have effects that intrude on other areas of the pastoral relationship with the congregation—simple lies, a refusal to admit mistakes, isolation of oneself, violation of confidentiality, depression, and sexual misconduct, for example. Masks undercut and eventually destroy the foundation of credibility Barnabas found so necessary to faithful ministry.

Barnabas stood with Saul in introducing him to the church in Jerusalem. In a different way, this "standing with" became important in Antioch (Acts 11:19-24). When Cypriot and Cyrenian disciples escaping persecution brought the good news to Antioch, the response was surprising. As they preached in the synagogue and taught their fellow Jews, the gospel met with both success and resistance—a pattern that became the norm for Luke's story. In one of those strange twists God's grace so often brings to our efforts, the gospel was heard and accepted with enthusiasm by Gentiles. But this success led to a problem, which in Acts 15 resulted in the Council of Jerusalem. By definition, Gentiles were unclean; that is, not Jewish and nonobservant of Jewish law. Contact with a Gentile tainted an observant Jew and made a period of purification necessary before the Jew could resume normal life. Because the church was at this point a Jewish sect, Gentiles remained outsiders. But one category of Gentiles was accepted by Jews as "God-fearers." Their search for faith led them to Jewish Scripture and the Jewish revelation of a single God who created all things and who remained deeply involved in guiding human history. Nonetheless, even these God-fearers could not be considered God's "chosen people." They remained Gentiles, unclean, and could not be fully accepted by the community of the faithful until they completed a purposely discouraging process of conversion (including the rite of circumcision). Few completed the process.[1]

Given the presence of "God-fearing" Gentiles participating on the fringes of Jewish life, it is likely that the missionaries' first success with Gentiles occurred among these God-fearers. But even these believing Gentiles still faced the barriers of the law and the deep prejudice that the majority of Jews held against them. Barnabas was sent to evaluate the situation in Antioch. To remain in good standing with Jewish law, Barnabas should have turned away from the Gentiles and confined the church's mission to his fellow Jews. Instead he took a step that had profound significance not only for his own ministry—a ministry soon shared by Saul—but for the future of the entire church. He continued to share the good news and to stand with all, including Gentiles, who heard and accepted the gospel.

Barnabas' decision and the Gentile response brought repercussions of anger and resistance. The ministry to Gentiles was challenged by other Jewish Christians who held a deep concern for maintaining the Mosaic Torah and who were offended by the inclusion of non-Jews in the gospel invitation. Barnabas and Paul (who, as described in the previous chapter, had become the lead partner of the pair) were appointed to give a defense of their ministry with Gentiles. This story, found in Acts 15, is perhaps the pivotal moment in the history of the church. Paul and Barnabas continued to stand firm in their conviction that the gospel is intended for all people, and they were given surprise support from Peter, who experienced his own epiphany regarding Gentiles.

As Acts 10 relates, Peter has a vision while resting on the roof of a house where he is visiting. Three times, a sheet containing a variety of animals classed unclean by Jewish dietary laws is lowered from heaven. A voice tells Peter to make a meal from these animals and, when Peter refuses ("Surely not, Lord! I have never eaten that which is unclean"), the voice announces, "What I have made clean, you must not call unclean." This vision is rapidly followed by the arrival of servants from the house of Cornelius, a Roman centurion and God-fearer, who has had his own vision. Cornelius has been instructed to find a man called Peter and to send for him. When Peter arrives at Cornelius' household, he is led by his rooftop vision to preach the gospel to the centurion and his entire household. When they, too, receive the gift of the Holy Spirit, Peter baptizes the whole household into the Christian faith.

Peter's story supported the defense given by Paul and Barnabas for their mission among Antioch's Gentiles: it was an undeniable reality that Gentiles received the Spirit of Christ just as Christ's Jewish followers did. The conclusion all three drew was that Gentiles must therefore be accepted as equals in Christ. Their testimony was persuasive to the Council (although Paul's letters reveal that the issue was far from settled), and Gentiles were received into the community with only a few further requirements. Standing with the outsider became a revelation of the universal intent of God's salvation and call.

Encouragement as Hospitality

Openness to outcasts and outsiders is an expression of scriptural hospitality. Scriptural hospitality is rooted in the nomadic traditions of the Hebrew tribes, in which travelers on long journeys relied on the welcome of others for protection and nourishment. New Testament scholar Bruce Malina describes biblical hospitality as "receiving outsiders and changing them from strangers to guests."[2] Although by New Testament times hospitality was less often a matter of life and death, it still was central to social interplay; we read, for example, in Luke 7:36-50, that Jesus is critical of Simon the Pharisee for neglecting his proper welcome. Proper hospitality included the mutual greeting and honoring of guest and host, offering and accepting refreshment and nourishment, and (the point at which the stranger became the guest) the washing of feet (see Genesis 18:4; 19:2; and 24:32, as well as John 13:1-20). The acceptance of hospitality is also important in Scripture. When Jesus sends out his disciples on their mission, he instructs them to depend on the hospitality of those they visit (Luke 10:4-12), and Paul also often relies on the hospitality of others (Acts 16:14-15; 18:1-3; 21:4, 7, 15).

"Receiving outsiders and changing them from strangers to guests" is a good definition for hospitality in the church as well. Of course we need also to be open and welcoming to those already a part of our congregations and to care for their spiritual and physical needs. But openness to members is considered part of the job description; we are expected to care for and stand with each other, even "difficult" members. But both pastors and lay leaders are sometimes criticized for "taking away time" from the needs of the congregation to offer care to people perceived as outsiders—particularly those who do not fit the congregation's perception of potential members. Encouraging hospitality toward outsiders can become a reminder that the church is to be, first and foremost, in mission.

Standing with Congregational "Outsiders"

When we speak of "outsiders" in relation to the church, we most likely have nonmembers in mind. This is obviously an important group to reach, but when we focus only on this population, we overlook a large source of untapped energy and ideas. Virtually every church I know has a significant percentage of inactive and underutilized members, people who have already made a commitment to Christ but have not yet found a place within the congregation to fulfill this pledge. Sometimes these members are fairly new and have been inadequately integrated into church life. Some regularly attend and give financial support to the church but do not participate in planning and doing ministry in the church's name. Some are attempting to deal with wounds suffered in their current or previous congregation. Some are on the membership rolls but have not yet found a way to contribute within the church's current ministry.

Barnabas' experience with Saul and later with the "God-fearing" Gentiles of Antioch suggests that the potential for dynamic ministry may exist within those who feel disconnected from the congregation or excluded from the inner circle of leadership. Certainly some people are happy simply to attend worship; others have been so damaged by church conflict or have felt left out for so long that they no longer seek to reconnect with a congregation, although they see no reason to drop their membership altogether. But many people who have lingered on the fringes are in fact eager to be asked to help in ministry. Although the pastor and current lay leaders may resist inviting "outsiders" into the mix, the inclusion of new and previously inactive members (even nonmembers) in church councils, planning teams, and the activities they plan often leads to both new ideas and new commitments to ministry.

How do we include those outside the circle in the full range of our ministry? How can we become hospitable to these members of Christ's body who feel less than fully included? Two publications I have found helpful in dealing with the larger questions of assimilation and inclusion are *The Inviting Church* by Roy Oswald and Speed Leas and *How to Live with Diversity in the Local Church* by Stephen Kliewer. Oswald and Leas's book reminds church leaders that the ability to grow and, more important, to enable new members to fulfill their ministry productively, requires that a congregation have a clear sense of its identity and mission and a plan for growth and assimilation. Kliewer defines the positive and negative aspects of diversity—which will exist in any church simply through the diversity of individuals—and gives practical advice on preparing for the opportunities for growth and conflict that diversity brings to a congregation. What concerns me directly in this section is the role of congregational leaders—lay and clergy—in creating an atmosphere that invites *all* the members and friends of the church to find and claim a role in its ministry.[3]

The first step is often to examine and understand congregational assumptions and patterns that have helped distance people—unwittingly or deliberately—from participation in the church's ministry. One such assumption I have heard from both clergy colleagues and lay leaders is that new members prefer not to be asked too soon to become involved in activities. This assumption often leads to our not asking them to become involved at all. Another assumption is that the elements that originally led someone to become inactive—a run-in with another member or a former pastor, for example—are still in effect. Often the anger or hurt from the original incident has faded; what keeps the inactive member inactive is the lack of an effort on the church's part to reconcile. When the congregation shows no interest in inviting someone back into participation, the inactive one is not likely to initiate participation on his or her own.

We often assume that inactivity in the church accurately reflects a person's attitude toward the church, if not toward God. While this may often be true, in my experience many inactive members are not critical of the congregation at all; they speak highly and with some nostalgia of the time when they were active. Many follow a disciplined devotional life and take seriously their discipleship in the workplace and community. The congregation and pastor are not always at fault in a member's decision to withdraw participation—sometimes people do not understand or are not properly trained in what commitment is expected of them as members, or they simply "get out of the habit" of attending and participating. Where the congregation and pastor may fail is in allowing people to withdraw without letting them know they are missed or without checking to see if there is a problem that can be resolved before inactivity takes root.

In all these assumptions—that people may be put off by commitment, that wounds exist and aren't healed, that inactivity inevitably means discontent or lack of interest—we need to begin by remembering that these are just *assumptions*. Acting on these assumptions as though they were proven fact can cause church leaders to narrow their vision to a small circle of people they see as dependable, allowing ministry to continue in the same way under the same leadership year after year. Unchanging vision and leadership can discourage new people from offering their gifts and can cause stagnation in the church's ministry. The leaders who continue to serve year after year may suffer from burnout, or they may form cliques to keep ministry under their control. The role of the encouraging pastor and lay leaders is to question assumptions about inactive or underactive members and to do so in a way that encourages both the pastor and active members to attempt to reconnect with members who have become inactive or who feel left on the outside. When "outsiders" are approached by people ready to listen to their stories and to encourage their participation, the discovery is often made that the "outsider" was never asked to be involved in any way other than to worship and to write checks. At other times, such approaches encourage old hurts or disappointments to surface, creating an opportunity for reconciliation. The point is that an encouraging pastor and laypeople must ask why and make possible an honest and welcoming exploration of the member's reasons for inactivity.

Needless to say, applying guilt for past inactivity should not be a part of this exploration. Those who have been outside the circles of leadership or active membership may already feel apologetic about their nonparticipation, or they may be angry or discouraged about feeling forced out or ignored. Scolding the church's outsiders, even playfully, will only deepen hard feelings and reinforce a reluctance to return. If a sensitive and thoughtful membership committee is already in place, this task seems logical work for them. If not, the pastor and lay leaders should recruit and provide training for a small and empathetic group of listeners to visit, hear without judging, and offer prayer with outsider members. When one of these trained visitors discovers that a pastoral call is needed or might be helpful, the pastor should follow up, but the work is much more effective if concerned laity are the primary caregivers. Inactive or underactive members often believe that such contacts are just part of the pastor's job, whereas contact from a layperson shows real concern and commitment on the church's part. Such encounters do not offer guarantees, of course. The inactive member's response may be "Thanks, but no thanks," or may yield promises of participation that are never fulfilled. *We cannot take responsibility for the member's response.* We can only patiently leave the door open, periodically renewing our invitation, and praying for reconciliation and healing when they are needed. We must make the offer to welcome those who have become outsiders, so they might return as friends. These *are* our responsibilities.

The process of reclaiming inactive members or involving members who feel themselves on the outside looking in can be lengthy, and it requires both time and energy—listening well is real work. Sometimes it may be difficult to avoid judgmental thoughts: "Why bother? After all, they are the ones who left us." We would have to look far to find a 21st-century church that had more variety and intensity of conflict than the church in Corinth, and only a little imagination is needed to hear some of the Corinthians saying about some of their brothers and sisters: "Let them go! We will be a more peaceful [or purer or less divided] church without them." It was to this divided, factional congregation that Paul wrote these words:

> We were baptized into one body in a single Spirit . . . and we were all given the same Spirit to drink. . . . If the foot were to say, "I am not a hand and so I do not belong to the body," it does not belong to the body any less for that. . . . As it is, the parts are many but the body is one. The eye cannot say to the hand, "I have no need of you," nor can the head say to the feet, "I have no need of you. . . . If one part is hurt, all the parts share its pain. And if one part is honored, all the parts share its joy. (1 Cor. 12:13, 15, 20-21, 26)

Too often, we forget that we do not pick and choose the members of our church. Rather, God has called us into the Body of Christ, a community of mutual love and accountability. When we allow a breach to remain unhealed or allow someone to slide from our view without discovering and fulfilling the ministry for which God has equipped her, we diminish ourselves and the congregation of which we are a part.

When a member has become inactive because of conflict or injury, we need also to remember that the church is called to be a community of reconciliation. (The fullest expression of this call is 2 Corinthians 5:14-21. See also Matthew 5:23-24 and Ephesians 2:11-18, where the emphasis is on reconciliation between Gentile and Jew.) The work of reconciliation may be difficult and painful, and the result may be to acknowledge the reality of separation and to encourage the member to move to a new church home rather than to return the member to activity in our own congregation. Still, the fact that the job is difficult does not relieve us of the responsibility to offer our time and concern and prayers.

Standing with Children

Inactive and underactive members are not the only people on the outside looking in. Many pastors and church boards speak of the importance of ministry to and for children but have little or no personal contact with the children of their own congregation, outside of the "children's moments" in a worship service. Pastors likely spend even less time with the children of their congregation than they do with the larger community beyond the congregation. How can the pastor and members be truly hospitable to children? How can we help children feel less like strangers in church and more like guests, even family?

Hospitality begins with taking children seriously as people. At a minimum, pastors and laypeople who do not regularly work with children should make the effort to know their names. Learning children's names as you learn their parents' takes little extra effort, and families notice both the effort and the lack of it. Making time to speak with and listen to the children as well as the adults of your church will help you learn how the church is and is not meeting children's needs. Conversations with children can take place in the hallways outside church-school classes or at church-sponsored latchkey programs. The church will also benefit greatly from having a pastor and a group of lay leaders who stay aware of events for children happening in the community (or are willing to create them) and who will take the time to connect with the children participating. As you share time with children, listen to what they enjoy, what bothers them, what makes them curious, with the same care you take to hear adults. (If you are just beginning involvement with children, speak naturally with them—it is better to start off using words a bit beyond their age range and adjust as you learn appropriate language than it is to talk down to them. If this is a skill you do not have but would like to learn, enjoy your first contacts with children in the company of someone who knows them well.)

As you make these connections and begin to know children, take them seriously as children of God who are ready to grow in faith. If children's moments are a part of your worship, shift them away from displays of the children's cuteness or thinly disguised sermon summaries for adults. Instead, use them to teach the basics of prayer or to introduce the children to the stories of Scripture; don't assume your church school curriculum is teaching them how to read and know Scripture—it often does not. Use children's moments to answer questions the children have about God or Jesus or the church. (Their parents can often help you discover these questions and will be grateful that another adult is willing to answer them.)

Children often feel disconnected from worship once the children's moments are over. If your service includes a time for prayer concerns, make room for the children to voice theirs. You might ask children to help write a congregational prayer for the following week, perhaps one of thanksgiving or one that celebrates the greatness of God. If the sermon can include illustrations from the children's experience, it will help them hear how God's word is meant for them, too. When the sermon emphasis makes this difficult, perhaps the pastor can work with parents or other laypeople to develop bulletin activities that connect the message with children's interests and needs. Many mission projects have made themselves child-friendly and can offer moments for emphasis during the service—the Heifer Project, Church World Service blankets, and denominational relief projects all demonstrate concrete ways our giving can help others. Older children can often be included in worship as singers, dancers, readers, and prayer leaders, as well as acolytes. Some adults have real difficulty when children are restless in worship; help them understand why it is important that children share in worship with the congregation. When children do become restless in worship, it helps to have bulletin supplements or drawing materials available to help channel their energy. Perhaps some adults could help as unofficial grandparents, taking the younger ones for walks or offering quiet playthings as distractions, so the parents are not alone in dealing with their restlessness.

In my current setting, one of our most effective community ministries is a Christian preschool and day-care facility. Some of the children who attend have a home church, in some cases our own; many do not. I meet once a week for chapel with each of the two preschool programs and with the after-school day-care group. This setting offers a wonderful opportunity for evangelism in its original sense of sharing good news. Chapel lasts from 10 to 15 minutes, and we do one or more of the activities mentioned in the previous paragraph during each chapel time.

For many of the children, this is the only time during the week they hear of a loving God who created them and cares for them. This is sufficient reason for my commitment of time, but chapel time has created other opportunities for ministry. Even families who have not yet heard the call to faith, or are not ready to participate in a church, know and greet me as "Pastor Paul." They ask for prayers and pastoral visits in crisis, and they share their children's triumphs and problems. The benefits to our congregation have been great as well—nearly two-thirds of our new members in the past three years have come to us through their contact with the preschool and day care. As these new members became involved, young families who had previously been inactive or sporadically active noticed the new energy in the church—sometimes by word of mouth, sometimes by attending—and became involved again. I have been blessed by this investment of time as well—by the challenge of answering difficult questions, by learning to express my faith in simple and concrete ways, and by the genuine love and prayers the children offer me.

Our members have also begun to take an active role in connecting with the children. In our worship service we share the prayer concerns voiced by the children during chapel. Our unit of United Methodist Women adopts day-care families during holidays and helps host the Harvest Day festival we hold for the preschool in October. The United Methodist Men bake welcome-back cookies for every day-care family in September. Three members of the congregation volunteer three days or more per week as teachers' aides. We have been reminded that our ministry with children can mean more than offering space.

Standing with Outcasts

Ministry and hospitality to the outcast are an important theme in Scripture. Both the law and the prophets showed concern for the widowed and orphaned, the alien, the oppressed—people who could not support and defend themselves and therefore were likely to suffer at the hands of others. The third-year tithe (Deut. 14:28-29; 26:12-15) and sabbatical year remission of debts (Deut. 15:1-11) are representative of the Torah's concern for the poor and oppressed. Next to idolatry and faithlessness to God, neglect and oppression of the powerless was the sin most decried by the prophets (Micah 3:1-4, Habakkuk 2:5ff., and Isaiah 10:1-4 and 58:1-5 all demonstrate this concern), and inclusion of the poor and outcast in salvation is a major component in the prophets' vision of the healing of creation (Zephaniah 3:14-20, Isaiah 58:6-14, and Isaiah 61 are examples of this promise and may be precedents to Jesus' parable of the last judgment in Matthew 25:31-46). Certainly Jesus' attention and commitment to sinners; to lame and blind people, and those with leprosy; and to women and children—all outcasts of his time—provide a model of compassion for those who call themselves his disciples. We are not exempt from the call to reach in compassion to outcasts, although our outcasts have changed from Jesus' time. A good working definition of a modern outcast is any person or group of people who bring such discomfort to you or your congregation that you resist including them in your ministry. While the definition of "outcast" will vary from church to church, I will offer thoughts on two such groups that have disturbed congregations I have served—poor people and gay and lesbian people.

Standing with the Poor

A constant challenge for congregations, particularly those whose membership is largely middle-class, is to do ministry with poor people. Poor families and individuals rarely receive true hospitality from the church, particularly if they are of a race different from the dominant race in the congregation. Ministry tends to be less *with* the poor than *for* the poor and usually comes in the form of food pantries and emergency help—ministry that requires poor people to come to the church or other agency to receive the help we choose to give them, and that insulates most members from contact with those we help. Too often our attitude toward poor people is at best paternal ("We know better than they do what they need; after all, they are poor and coming to us for help!") or even less helpfully, judgmental ("If they are poor, they must deserve to be"). We want to be certain that the help we offer goes where it will be truly helpful, but our efforts to do so often look and feel very much like mistrust and a need to control. To prevent misuse, we may find it necessary to see the driver's license and income verification of an individual who uses the food pantry, but the attitude we bring to the request and our willingness to hear the individual's story as we make the request will define whether the client experiences the encounter as loving or depersonalizing. Without true concern for the one we help, our outreach will likely not be an encounter where good news is heard and healing is offered; it may become just another set of rules and hoops. How do we move from stranger (or "client") to guest?

The need to provide hospitality as well as help led First United Methodist to move the food pantry from the church basement into the community center two blocks up the street. The variety of activities taking place at the center makes the reason for the pantry participants' visits less obvious. Participants are greeted with a cup of coffee and encouraged, while they wait to be served, to see what else is happening at the center. The center receptionist or another volunteer is available to listen, and pantry users are invited to join others in the prayer room. If someone voices an emotional or spiritual need, the receptionist or volunteer may refer that client to the center's licensed counselor or one of the community clergy. Children who come with parents to the pantry have space to play and, usually, someone to join them in play while the parent is in conversation or loading food.

When we listen to what those who are poor have to suggest about services we provide, we recognize them as individuals who have insights and gifts to share with us and to help us improve those services. Through such listening, the board of directors for Neighborhood Services, the community center serving the area surrounding the Ohio State University campus, began training clients of the center to administer the pantry and clothing centers themselves. This arrangement gave the clients a way to reciprocate for services received, as well as providing work experience for future job applications. The churches that participate in the Mount Sterling Community Center have begun to host spiritual-growth classes and opportunities for group prayer at the center to accompany the exercise classes and training in basic finance. As we listen, we may discover that participants have a skill they could teach or that could begin an interest group for others in the community. If we truly respect and truly hear the people we serve, we can help them develop the gifts they have—gifts they could share.

Standing with Gay and Lesbian People

The issue of ministry with gay men and lesbians is a difficult one that will almost certainly raise painful questions in a congregation. Not all congregations will be called to consider it, and there will almost certainly be conflict when the opportunity for ministry arises. I don't have a detailed program to suggest, but I do believe that gay and lesbian people are called by Christ, although pastors and congregations often treat them the way middle- and upper-class congregations often treat poor people—as though they are our "Gentiles," people to be kept firmly on the outside rather than as people who recognize and receive God's grace. When we are given an opportunity to be

Christ to gay people, I believe we can do better than the "hate the sin, love the sinner" approach that often seems unloving, even hateful, to those on the receiving end.

Are those gay or lesbian people "sinners"? Of course they are. So is everyone else in our pews and pulpits. Should they be expected to confront their sinfulness? Certainly. But heterosexual Christians often believe that homosexual Christians are greater sinners than the rest of the population. Too often the church's approach to gay and lesbian seekers goes something like this: "We will share the good news you need to know once you let go of your sin. We do this rather than simply bringing the good news and trusting Christ's word and the Spirit's power to bring needed transformation." What if we took the same approach to other forms of human sinfulness that we take to sexual sin in its many forms? We could ban the angry or the gluttonous or the gossipy or the self-righteous from our congregations until they had ceased to practice their sin—all of these are sins declared dangerous to our life together as followers of Christ, and all of these receive more attention in Scripture than does homosexuality. We could ban those who practice these sins, but I suspect that both our pulpits and our pews would be much emptier if we did.

At Summit United Methodist Church in Columbus, Ohio, we had an active AIDS ministry that brought a number of gay and lesbian people to our worship services and then into membership. One of the older members stopped me after a service one day to say, "I don't understand what these people do in the bedroom, and I don't approve of it." As I waited for the "they go or I go" that I expected, Walter went on, "But if we don't let them hear about Jesus' love for them in his church, how can we expect them to hear about it at all?" Whatever form a given church's ministry takes toward gay and lesbian people, it strikes me that Walter's insight is a wonderful starting point. Outcasts are given to us to love in Christ's name, not to change in Christ's name. If we show Christ's love wholeheartedly and people receive Christ's love wholeheartedly, we can trust the transforming power of the Holy Spirit to bring whatever changes are needed—to us as well as to the outcast. This is not simply cheap grace. Christ's love comes to us just as we are, but it never leaves us just as we are, and the changes we are called to make are often at the place closest to our hearts—the rich young ruler and Zacchaeus, Saul and Peter serve as powerful demonstrations of Christ's transforming love at work.

Reducing Barriers to Ministry

Referring to the people with whom we minister as "outcasts" might seem unnecessarily negative. Remember the definition I offered earlier of modern outcasts, however. The issue is our discomfort, not the unacceptability of the other person. The reality is that all churches erect barriers that block ministry to certain groups, creating racial, economic, sexual, or other kinds of outcasts. The most difficult barriers to overcome may be theological, may concern church government, or may involve the way we express our faith in worship. Some of these barriers are raised around our understanding and practice of the sacraments. Infant baptism is one dividing line, transubstantiation another. Some denominations and congregations limit communion to members, and others have an open-table policy. Another barrier is raised around the ordination of women. Other barriers have to do with salvation itself; those who are not within the denomination or sect are considered lost. These barriers are made obvious by those "inside," though they are not so easily understood by those outside the barrier. Other barriers are more subtle. People who wish to see the gospel applied to social issues may feel themselves outsiders in a congregation whose individual evangelism and salvation are the sole concerns, or whose passion and energy are reserved for the new building project. Sadly, worship style can create outsiders in a congregation when one style is elevated above another as "the way to do it." These are all legitimate differences, but we often make them barriers by the way we communicate and emphasize our dissimilarities. Confronting any of these barriers will bring painful conflict. But if we are to welcome all people in Christ's name, we need to push at these barriers and, with the help of the Spirit, discover ways over and through them.

Reflections

1. What members are left out of your congregation's ministry and why?

   - In what ways do you currently reach out to members outside the circle?
   - What steps does your congregation take to welcome and include new members in your congregation and ministries?
   - How familiar are you with the history of your congregation? How can you learn more?
   - What steps can you take to connect with inactive members?
   - Who might be willing to learn and use the skills needed to reach out to those outside your active membership?

2. How open are you to investing your own time and love in the children of your congregation and community?

   - If this "standing with" seems intimidating to you, who are some people who can help you take your first steps?
   - Ask for help in evaluating your contacts with children; look for honest feedback.

- Who in the congregation enjoys working with children and can help the congregation create an environment that children will experience as more hospitable?

3. I used poor people and gay people as examples of standing with outcasts.
   - What outcasts have come to your congregation in the past year and why?
   - How have you shown hospitality to those you consider outcasts and outsiders?
   - How have you encouraged others to receive their outcasts and outsiders?
   - Who in the congregation has helped you or could help you grow in hospitality?

FOUR

Standing against Fear

The Ministry of Courage

Then some Jews arrived from Antioch and Iconium and turned the people against them. They stoned Paul and dragged him outside the town, thinking he was dead. The disciples came crowding around him but, as they did so, he stood up and went back to the town. The next day he and Barnabas left for Derbe.—Acts 14:19-20

IN THE PAST TWO CHAPTERS, I have referred to resistance to change in ministry by those experiencing change both in the framework we use for ministry and in the vision we have for reaching people outside our congregation. Resistance is shown not only by members of congregations where change is taking place; honesty compels me to admit that the resistance to change I experience within myself as pastor can be fierce. My resistance can come from factors as mundane as not wanting to deal with the detail work of change—the letters to be written and mailed, the meetings to get everyone on board and participating, the changes in schedule or routine I might have to make. Sometimes, though, my resistance comes from deeper within; I don't really want to deal with the resistance of others, and I find myself anticipating criticism (and even resenting it in advance). While we may not find anything frightening in the idea of encouragement, in my experience the greatest enemy of the ministry of encouragement is often fear.

During many of the crucial moments in Barnabas' ministry, he had to deal with fear. (In fact, I believe the entire book of Acts can be seen as a struggle for the truth of the gospel against human fearfulness.) As we have seen, Barnabas' partnership with Saul really began when Barnabas spoke to the apostles on behalf of the church's former persecutor. In that case, the church had a valid reason for fear. Saul had been enthusiastic in his pursuit and persecution of those following Christ, and the consequences for those he captured had been grave—imprisonment, forfeiture of property, even death. The problem with even this legitimate fear was that it blinded the apostles to a new reality: Saul had changed. Saul had become one of them. Saul was speaking for Christ, and the genuine commitment of his work had been confirmed by the fruit of new converts. By speaking for Saul and against fear, Barnabas made it possible for this new reality to reshape the apostles' view of Saul, allowing them to support Saul in his ministry.

Acts 14:1-20 reminds us that Paul and Barnabas had to overcome personal fear to fulfill their ministry. During their journeys together, the pair faced resistance from Jews who were unpersuaded by the gospel and hostile to it. They also encountered resistance from Jewish Christians who were convinced of the truth of the gospel but could not understand or accept that this good news was to be shared with Gentiles. As Acts 14 shows, Paul and Barnabas met resistance from civil authorities in Lycaonia, and they would face more such resistance in the future. Both Roman and Jewish leaders responded to the gospel with hostility when reaction to the Word created civil disorder or challenged cherished cultural customs and attitudes. (See Acts

19:23ff., a description of the riot of Ephesian silversmiths, for a description of such an incident.) Although Lycaonia was not the only location where resistance took the form of a physical threat to the missionaries, it was one of the most serious. Paul was nearly killed when the crowd turned on the pair and stoned him.

Repeatedly in Luke's narrative about the church, fear plays a major role in resistance to the gospel. The reason for the apostles' fear of Saul is clear. The reality of his persecution and physical threat justified their fear. When Peter and John are brought before the Sanhedrin after ignoring the Temple Council's ban on preaching and healing in Christ's name (Acts 5:17-42), they confound their accusers by maintaining the truth of the gospel. Saul's old teacher Gamaliel offers some profound advice to the assembled council:

> What I suggest . . . is that you leave these men alone and let them go. If this enterprise, this movement of theirs, is of human origin it will break up of its own accord; but if it does in fact come from God you will be unable to destroy them. Take care not to find yourselves fighting against God. (Acts 5:38-9)

But after initially following Gamaliel's advice, the authorities in Jerusalem—and in town after town visited by the apostles—are unable to do so in the long term. Instead, they continue to attack and persecute Paul and Barnabas and others who follow the Way. While the motives of these authorities are mixed, at least a part of their reaction stems from fear—fear of change, fear that their way of life is being threatened, fear of being asked to go where they are not prepared to go, perhaps fear that they might be wrong, that Jesus had indeed risen. Acting out of fear and hostility, the temple authorities attempt to suppress the teaching and preaching of God's new Word because the good news it offers challenges their authority and control. (The resistance to Barnabas' and Paul's work in Antioch that resulted in the Council of Jerusalem may have arisen from a similar mixture of theological disagreement and fear on the part of Jewish Christians.)

We are mistaken if we assume that Barnabas and Paul did not wrestle with fears similar to those of their opponents. Both were brought up in a life observant of Torah; both were raised to think of themselves as belonging to God's chosen people, who lived faithfully in a world gone awry through the power of sin. As Paul testifies in his letter to the Philippians, he was not only raised as a Jew; he was trained as a Pharisee (Phil. 3:3-7). So both Barnabas and Paul would have had to confront the fact that their call was taking them outside the commitment and way of life they had known and loved and trusted, that they might spread a new Word. How could they have not felt fear?

Against divisive fear, their own and that of others, Barnabas and Paul could only maintain faith in the evidence of Scripture and the presence of the Spirit in the lives of Gentile Christians. As we know from the theological disputes of our own time, appeal to Scripture does not always remove ambiguity. All sides in church controversies routinely search for and fervently apply texts that support their positions. Those who opposed sharing the gospel with Gentiles may have referred to Torah purity injunctions or to the royal promises made to the descendants of David that God would call the nations through them. Nor can the presence of the Spirit of truth be unambiguously seen or measured by those seeking truth. The reality is that conflict and disagreement within the church are as messy and difficult to resolve as conflict outside it. With some conflicts, only the passage of time and the fruit of a decision will disclose the truth. (Paul's clashes with the Judaizers were never clearly resolved in Paul's lifetime.) Our own culture's battles over slavery; the role of women in the church; and the proper response of the church to war, terrorism, and genocide should remind us to proceed with appropriate humility in claiming exclusive truth for our own viewpoint. This humility does not, however, relieve us of the burden of grappling with God's Word and opening ourselves to the movement of the Spirit as we search out our way. Perhaps we should more readily apply Gamaliel's advice and approach conflict with patience and love for our opponents and trust God to help us sort out our proper response to problems in God's own time and way. What is clear from the model of Barnabas is that we cannot—either as pastors or congregations—resist change simply because we fear negative response or conflict.

Pastoral Fear in Ministry

One difficulty I may have in approaching the problem of fear in ministry is my reluctance to admit that the fear exists. If I acknowledge that fear affects me, I may believe that I am confessing to a lack of faith or that I am admitting a weakness or character flaw. One way I can avoid acknowledging my fear is to call it something else. Hence, we have many books written for the Christian or pastor experiencing *stress*. Certainly, stress is a reality; just as certainly, fear is a large part of stress. Jack Harris, in *Stress, Power, and Ministry*, makes a clear connection between fear and stress for both pastor and congregation, including this frank statement:

> [M]ost of us expend tremendous energy walling off our fear, shielding ourselves against vulnerability in any form while investing someone or something external to ourselves—our passions, our wealth, our status, our physical vitality, our analyst, our family, God—with the power to protect us from pain and death.[1]

To Harris's list of protectors, we might add that congregations and pastors often look for the same protection and reassurance from each other. Books and counseling that help us deal with stress inevitably force us to confront fear, no matter by what name we call it. We may speak of apprehension or anxiety or tension or use a variety of other alternative words, but we cannot escape the simple fact demonstrated in Acts and other passages from Scripture. Dealing with fear is a part of our spiritual journey.

In a variety of settings, both laypeople and colleagues have asked me: How can we experience fear if we truly trust God? But certainly there is plenty of witness in Scripture that people of faith do feel fear. Many of the psalms (Psalms 22 and 88 come to mind immediately) are songs of a fearful person seeking God's presence and support in a time of fear, and the problem of fear is not always resolved by psalm's end. (Psalm 22 looks forward to God's answer and affirms God's righteousness, but Psalm 88 continues in a tone of anguish and despair and concludes, "The darkness is my closest friend." Other psalms express more ambiguity than these. The psalmist remains under assault from enemies—which may include both other people and the psalmist's own flaws—but hoping that God will offer rescue. See Psalms 38, 55, and 137 for this mixture of hope and struggle.) Luke's Gospel is clear that the experience of the risen Christ brought fear as well as joy to those who saw him (Luke 24:37). Even if it is not explicitly stated, it would hardly be surprising if, in Acts 9, Ananias feared going to heal the blinded Saul, and we can be fairly certain that Barnabas and Paul felt some twinge of fear as they were physically assaulted by the crowds in Lycaonia. Faithfulness does not mean being free of fear; it means trusting God and continuing God's work despite fear.

What are some of the fears that affect our ministries? The first fear we might name is the *fear of change*. Pastors often identify as a frustration a congregation's reluctance to try new ways of reaching out or learning. A fairly common complaint in discussions among pastors is that a certain methodological principle crosses all denominational lines: "But we've always done it that way!" Many congregations do resist change and come to it reluctantly, if at all. But the implication of this complaint—that pastors are champing at the bit to introduce invigorating change into a church's ministry, only to be held back by resistance from the laity—is sometimes self-serving and inaccurate. Pastors are as likely to resist change as are congregations, particularly if the change is introduced by someone else or the potential change challenges the pastor's comfort zone. Fear of change is often *fear of losing control of a situation.* When pastors identify themselves or allow themselves to be identified as the sole or central starting point for a congregation's ideas and leadership, they may be particularly susceptible to such fear.

As First United Methodist began the exploration of Spirit-led ministry, as detailed in chapter 2, a fairly minor event reminded me of my own reluctance to let go of control. A member of our choir had asked, "Why do you use a manuscript to preach? You seem very comfortable preaching and don't use your notes all that much." As the conversation continued and I considered moving away from both manuscript and pulpit, I was startled by an uncomfortable fact. For most of my pastorate, I had tried to de-emphasize differences between pastor and laity in most aspects of ministry—avoiding the title "Reverend," encouraging the use of my first name, dressing casually, urging people to give no more weight to my contributions than to theirs in discussion. But I had maintained the differences in worship—dressing in alb and stole, remaining behind the pulpit during worship (except when leading children's moments), always having a pastoral prayer as part of the liturgy rather than allowing laypeople to use their gifts to lead shared prayer. The insight I could not avoid was that this formal approach to worship—and this insight is in my case only; I am not commenting on other pastors' worship style—came less from theological conviction than it did from a need to be in control. Standing in the pulpit, elevated above the worshipers, clad in my robe and referring to my manuscript gave me a security blanket. The unfortunate side effect was that my worship style worked against my leadership style, reinforcing the idea that I was somehow closer to God and on a higher level than laypeople. The day I moved to preach from floor level, in coat and tie rather than in my robe, and with only a few note cards, I felt a pang of fear. What if I forget what I want to say? Where will I hide if something goes wrong? My preparation for preaching has not changed, and I still have to do the work of exegesis and write out most of the sermon before distilling it as notes onto my four-by-six cards. Still, two years into the new preaching method, I remain uneasy at times. I have sympathy for Adam and Eve: "We were naked so we hid." (Again, I don't mean my personal experience to be taken as a comment on pastors who remain with the pulpit. The traditions of a congregation, the nature of the worship space, and the pastor's own style are just three of many factors that could affect this decision.)

Colleagues have affirmed that similar small changes in routine, particularly routines played out in public, cause them discomfort that is out of scale for the situation. Although some of us remain reluctant to use the word "fear" to describe our reaction, we usually agree that our discomfort has to do with a sense that we are no longer in control. This loss of control "worries" us or makes us "anxious." When changes affect our ministry in a larger sense, our discomfort and anxiety also rise in intensity. A friend and colleague serving as senior pastor in a growing suburban church experienced a true upheaval when he and the personnel committee made a change in the associate pastor's position. Rather than a young, less-experienced pastor whose focus was mainly on the youth groups of the church, they asked for and received a veteran pastor whose experience in pastoral calls and whose counseling and preaching skills created more of a co-pastor situation. The youth program became lay-led under the supervision of the education committee and went well almost immediately. However, the pastoral and lay leadership needed two years of constant attention and communication—with each other and the congregation as a whole—to establish the new job descriptions and responsibilities before the stress level began to subside and staff and congregation were able to begin working together in their new roles. Although this new relationship is bearing good fruit now, both my friend and his colleague acknowledge that the two years were their most stressful in ministry, an assessment shared by the congregation's lay leadership. Because the process was new, no one could control the direction or the outcome. One factor in their eventual success was the absolute commitment of the pastors and other leaders to communicate with each other throughout the process. Victories were celebrated as a source of strength and confirmation of their direction; problems were identified and worked through as they occurred rather than becoming a source of ongoing conflict. Was my friend pleased with the results? "Most definitely." Would he do it again? "Not on your life"—though this he said with a smile.

As the leadership of First UMC began to work together in the new process for discernment described in chapter 2, people close to me saw that I was experiencing a higher level of anxiety and irritation. Even though I was taking a leading role in assisting and interpreting the changes and could accept them intellectually, I felt increasingly out of sync with what was happening. I was not only having to talk about the equal importance of the ideas and gifts of laypeople; I was having to live those words out by giving up control—even the subtle (or less-than-subtle) control

I had previously allowed myself, my disapproving body language when discussion didn't go in the direction I preferred, my well-timed joke that deflated an idea I really didn't want to see put into action. My own discomfort was intensified by the difficulty some congregational leaders had in accepting and adjusting to the changes, and these leaders' consequent resistance. (As one of my readers pointed out, perhaps they too felt out of sync.) "Dread" is not too strong a word for my anticipation of and reaction to meetings as we began to rely less on my agenda and more on listening for the Spirit's agenda. The changes were taking me out of control. I don't mean control of the congregation, because I had come to Mount Sterling knowing that the congregation had good leadership and that members were able to generate their own ideas for ministry. Where I was losing control (so I thought) was in my own habits of leadership. I literally did not know what my role was to be in this process. I was concerned that I might lose credibility with the congregation if we spent several months on this process and found no clear direction for ministry. If I lost the confidence of the leadership, I was concerned for my future—not just in Mount Sterling but also for the impact a failure here might have on future pastoral appointments. It was not until the prayer groups began to help us discover that the Spirit did have a direction for us that I began to feel less fear for my future as pastor. Even more than two years into the process, though, I sometimes feel cut adrift from my comfort zone. I still find it odd to be asked a question about a ministry and have to answer: "I don't know. You probably need to ask ———— [the layperson coordinating]." I continue to be both pleased and startled when an opportunity for ministry opens in an unexpected direction or form. Our discussion of the need for classes in English as a second language (ESL) for the Mexican workers at a local plant appears to be growing into a van ministry to help this mostly Roman Catholic group to attend worship services in a nearby city.

Mixed with other types of fear may be a *fear of consequences*. What if attendance sags or members leave because I take a controversial stance on a social issue or commit an error in counseling a parishioner? What if leaders resign their positions or our big givers reduce their pledges in disapproval of my ministry? What if the personnel committee asks me to leave? While this is less of a concern now that I am starting my fifth year in Mount Sterling, these are real worries for many of my colleagues. One reason so many pastors feel vulnerable to consequences is a sense—accurate or not—that they are allowed very little space for mistakes or ineffectiveness. This fear can be eased somewhat by sympathetic or supportive denominational superiors. However, even in connectional systems like the United Methodist Church, where pastoral moves are initiated by a cabinet (made up of the bishop and district superintendents) rather than by individual congregations, very little can be done to keep people from voting against a pastor's leadership through nonattendance or withdrawal of financial support. When pastors cannot or do not develop a group of supportive colleagues or superiors, the sense of aloneness in their situation can quickly become oppressive.

Such a sense of loneliness and lack of support can lead the pastor to a crippling reaction. If I allow myself to set up a defensive wall against all criticism, I will likely find it difficult to admit a mistake or weakness, and nearly impossible to learn from justified and well-meant criticism. If I don't work through such defensiveness and overcome it, I may develop a *fear of weakness* or fear of *admitting* weakness. When I cannot admit a mistake or weakness, I cannot properly work through the effects of that mistake. I begin to find excuses or scapegoats to cover my own failings, so that my reluctance to accept and admit responsibility becomes precisely the kind of fatal weakness I am trying to avoid.

Although this may be considered a mistake of inexperienced pastors, many veteran pastors have learned to hide their fear and shift responsibility for their errors. They do not identify or understand their fear as such and therefore do not resolve it. The avoidance strategies they have learned will go with them from parish to parish until their effectiveness is destroyed and several churches have been made to suffer the consequences. Other pastors react to their fear in a different but equally destructive way. Rather than shifting responsibility for their errors, they overcompensate and accept more responsibility for ministry and its results than is really theirs. In this reaction, ministry is less a problem to be avoided than an ever-increasing burden. Those who blame others for their mistakes often have integrity issues similar to those I mentioned in the previous chapter—dishonesty, sexual misconduct, avoidance of difficult pastoral relationships. Those who take on too much responsibility are often affected by depression, illness, or a sense of inadequacy. Both reactions can lead to marital problems, addictions, and spiritual emptiness. Pastors in both categories often leave or are asked to leave parish ministry altogether.

Even more destructive to my ministry than a fear of consequences can be a sense that I am not properly fulfilling God's call to ministry. This *fear of failing God* can also eat away at a pastor's confidence. In my own experience, this fear is wrapped up with many of the symptoms already cited: a sense of being out of control, feeling under attack for mistakes I have made or for disagreements with congregational leaders, a sense that the responsibility of leadership is becoming too heavy. The difference between the fear of failing God and my other fears in relation to ministry is that I do not feel that this struggle is merely the normal conflict I can experience with congregational leaders, nor do I perceive it as a temporary problem that will be resolved as our shared ministry unfolds. Instead, I interpret this fear as a message from God, telling me that I am not listening, or that I am going in a direction God does not intend, or that I am simply no longer in touch with God's will for me. This self-doubt often leads to depression and anger and to a questioning of my vocation. Do I still belong in the ordained ministry? Have I ever belonged in this ministry?

Congregational Fear in Ministry

Because my experience in ministry for the past 20 years has been that of a pastor, I have less to say about the fears of a congregation, but congregational fear obviously can have a deep effect on a church's ministry. Yes, many congregations do fear change, and they respond to this fear with the same defensiveness pastors do. Many congregations have a deep distrust or *fear of pastors.* They feel betrayed by a former pastor or, worse, by a series of pastors. As a result they find it difficult to trust and work with pastoral leaders on even a basic level, affected by what we might call a "toxic" level of distrust. This distrust often spills over into relationships with other members—toxic congregations often split into factions—and can lead to a sense of powerlessness. To be sure, this fear may be connected to fear of losing control of the church's ministry, but congregations have often learned to fear pastors because of the dishonest or incompetent behavior of former pastors. In traditions such as my own, where a change in pastoral assignment is initiated by judicatory officials, members may fear developing a close relationship with a pastor or following a pastor's leadership in creating new ministry. (This fear may also occur in other traditions when a congregation has a reputation of being a "stepping-stone" church—one where the pastor stays a few years to gain experience before moving on to a larger, better-paying congregation.) What will happen when the pastor is moved? What if the change in pastors happens before change in ministry is complete or before the congregation has time to accept and make the change its own? Are we just going from change to change without coherent reasons for change? Why learn to trust someone who is such a temporary part of our church life?

As I spoke to laypeople about this topic, I was surprised to hear some of my own fears expressed in different ways. As we have worked through the process for discerning ministry at First Church, the lay members have often felt as unsure of our direction as I. One fear this uncertainty has raised for the laity is *fear of displacing the pastor.* This concern has been expressed negatively as, "Why should we do this? It's his job, not ours." (These words were used by one member asked to participate in the shepherding program that welcomed visitors and new members and linked them with other people and ministries within the church.) More often, this fear has been a sensitive concern that my ideas and opinions as pastor not be overlooked or that my ministry not be limited by the decisions of the lay council. This possibility was particularly a concern for those members who took initiative to begin the community center. The availability of the building, the signing of the lease, the moving of the food pantry—all these happened so quickly that all that was needed from me was encouragement and my signature on certain documents. As issues arose of finding funds, creating standards for building use, and increasing participation among non-United Methodists in the center, the center's board worried that I was not being involved enough in the decision making. More than once, I assured the members that I would be available for specific events or to help with specific decisions about the center but that I felt there were other nearby centers and other people within the community who could offer better counsel than I. This has indeed proved to be the case; the community center flourishes with a broad range of programs and a broad range of community involvement.

Earlier, I spoke of the fear of change we all face and the sometimes patronizing attitude pastors take toward congregational fear of change. A recent conversation with one of our laypeople helped me better understand one form this fear takes. For Bea, fear of change at the church is *fear of losing family.* She grew up in our church, her wedding took place in the church, and her children have been raised in its Sunday school and youth groups. When Bea suffered loss or when she could find no other place to turn, her church was her extended family. Even when Bea experienced a period of conflict as one of the church leaders, her distress at the conflict was magnified by her feeling that she was facing rejection from her church family. Bea's insight helped me understand the congregation's discomfort at accepting and including new members. Most of our members recognize that the young families coming to First Church represent the congregation's future and that they can inject new blood and new possibility into our leadership. But these newcomers are not really "ours." Some have roots in our community or towns nearby, but others are part of the growing bedroom-community population. Like adopted children or new in-laws, these newcomers are a part of the family but also are a "not yet." They haven't lived here before. They don't know our history, and some haven't yet shared the church's joys and pains. I suspect that, for some, these new families are a reminder of the children who have left the community or who remain but have left the church. When they suggest or support changes in worship, they are tampering with our rituals, much as the meddlesome in-law who suggests opening presents on Christmas Eve rather than Christmas morning. When they are included in a vote on renovation, they don't have the long-term attachment to the building or understand its history as do longer-term members.

Such deep feelings about the church need to be recognized and valued, because members who hold such feelings have made major contributions to the strength and appeal of our congregation. But these feelings also need to be balanced by intentional hospitality and inclusion, so that a newcomer does not become the in-law or adopted child who is never accepted as "really" family. The movement of hospitality from stranger to guest must be extended to become the movement from guest to brother or sister. In other words, fear of losing family cannot become a barrier to opening our hearts and arms to those who are seeking new life in Christ.

I don't believe that the ministry of encouragement is a cure-all for congregational fears. It is true that some congregations have reached the toxic levels of distrust I mentioned earlier—just as some pastors reach poisonous levels of dishonesty or incompetence—and need outside help, perhaps an outside consultant or interim pastor to help resolve their issues and regain the ability to trust their pastors and each other. But I do believe that the ministry of encouragement is a good place to begin. Such ministry builds on the strengths a congregation has, resists manufacturing the kind of quick fix the leadership may have previously been promised, and takes the focus off what the pastor has to offer and places it on what can be accomplished together, with the partnership of the Spirit.

Standing against Fear

As might be gathered by my earlier comments, I firmly believe that the first step in dealing with the "fear factor" in ministry is to recognize and admit its presence. We should not be surprised that fear exists in ministry. Whether we name the enemy as Satan or our own dark side or some other agency, Scripture and the experience of our spiritual ancestors tell us that the struggle against Christ's work will be fierce. Fear is a powerful weapon against ministry, particularly when the fear is our own. If we do not acknowledge our fear, if we try to cover it over or pretend it does not exist, fear, like unacknowledged conflict, will simply grow and assume power that it would not have if named and confronted. We need to accept fear as a reality and plan ways to confront and disarm it. We also need to admit our fear to others, so they can be in support of us in our struggle.

Not surprisingly, the struggle against fear begins with prayer. I have found the psalms invaluable in leading me through the maze of discouragement and gloom that fear can cause. They are a reminder that others have walked this maze and have come through to the affirmation of God's presence, love, and healing. They provide me with words when my own prayers lack focus or conviction. *"My God, my God, why have you forsaken me?"* are not only words for the cross. They can also be cried from an office or a darkened sanctuary, and the words that come later in Psalm 22, the passage Jesus quotes in his anguish— *"For he has not despised nor disregarded the poverty of the poor, has not turned away his face, but has listened to the cry for help"*—can also be whispered in hope or shouted in joy as we feel God's presence again. Other psalms can be prayed as affirmation of God's good gifts and for protection from fear. A close friend led me to Psalm 91 and its promise of protection. Psalm 139, with its reminder of God's constant presence and loving knowledge of me, has long been a favorite of mine, and Psalm 23 naturally leaps to mind when all other words fail me.

While my own grounding in prayer is a necessity for healthy ministry, I also depend on the prayers of the community. I continually ask for and receive my congregation's prayers. One of the units of our United Methodist Women's organization, the Rebecca Circle, has taken on the commitment to pray daily for me, my family, and my ministry. At times merely remembering that these 18 women are praying for me each day can help me change my focus from fear toward God's lovingkindness or rescue me from making a mistake or accepting the promises of temptation. In my ongoing battle with anger and depression—both of which feed on and are fed by fear—I have sought out specific opportunities for healing prayer and, through God's blessing, have received the healing I sought.

Support Groups

One of the great mistakes we make as pastors is to believe that we can work faithfully for Christ without the honest give-and-take of colleagues in ministry. Over and over again in Scripture, we are reminded that ministry is not to be a solitary activity. For every John the Baptist preaching and baptizing alone in the wilderness, there are numerous examples of partnership and support. Jesus' ministry was sustained by a circle of support, mostly women, who offered him hospitality in their homes and sometimes traveled with him, seeing to his daily needs. When Jesus sent out the 70 messengers to preach and heal, he sent them in pairs (Luke 10:1). The partnerships of Peter and John (Acts 3-4); Barnabas and Paul; Paul, Silas, and Timothy (Acts 15:36-18:22), are the norm for mission in Acts, while Philip's solo preaching in Samaria (Acts 8:5-8) and his later meeting with the Ethiopian seem to be exceptions to this pattern of partnership. Moses was advised by Jethro to share leadership (Exod. 18:13-27), and even Jeremiah had his Baruch, who took dictation of Jeremiah's prophecies and delivered them when Jeremiah was banned from the Temple (Jeremiah 36).

One of the great weapons against fear in ministry is a thoughtful, prayerful group of colleagues who meet regularly to care for each other's spiritual welfare. Much as the disciples crowded around Paul outside Lycaonia to offer him protection, these collegial groups offer us a place to voice and find healing for our own wounds. Ever present is the danger that these groups can become gossip circles and gripe-fests, so they need to be managed with care and attention for their real purpose. In my own group, each member is encouraged to speak of his or her achievements and struggles since the last meeting and to attend to each one's spiritual state (although we do not always use this language). We identify ongoing issues each of us has with his or her congregation, denomination, or self, and we share resources for prayer and study. And yes, we sometimes catch ourselves griping and gossiping and needing to pull ourselves back on track. This group has become a source of nourishment and occasionally a survival kit for all involved.

Collegial support groups should be supplemented with the support of leaders and listeners within the local congregation. These people should be chosen prayerfully, because not every parishioner wants to or should hear about the pastor's struggles. But such supporters can offer compassionate and honest criticism of a pastor's ministry and the effect it has within the congregation and community. They can help a pastor understand a congregation's story, including how pastor-parish relationships have worked in the past, and help the pastor understand how she or he is perceived. At the same time, laity can hear from the pastor how he or she perceives the congregation and how it feels to this pastor to serve in this setting. This group can help pastor and congregation reach a better level of mutual understanding and can provide a distant early warning system of potential misunderstandings and conflicts within the church. The group can also bring appropriate support to both pastor and congregation in case such problems or conflicts move from potential to actual. In asking for the support and insight such a group can offer, we must take care not to violate confidentiality or form cliques within the congregation; it is perhaps wise to limit social occasions with those who make up this support group.

Seeking Alternatives

Much pastoral fear comes when we feel trapped within a situation or by a conflict. Often the "trap" occurs because we are not able to see alternatives. In *Leadership in the Wesleyan Tradition,* Lovett Weems speaks of the "tyranny of the 'or.'" We reduce our options to either/or when there may be any number of alternatives. Weems points out that much of John Wesley's genius was in his ability to synthesize two or more conflicting viewpoints in a way that recognized the tension between them while finding the truth and insight into faithful living they shared.[2] Developing the prayerful discipline of finding the path out of "either/or" can help us avoid unnecessary conflict and reduce the need to win that creates so much avoidable and dangerous division within our entire culture, including our congregations. Either/or demands that one alternative be rejected in favor of the other; seeking common ground and creative alternatives makes it more likely that everyone involved is heard and can take ownership of the decision. Conflict can also be reduced if pastors and influential laity do not feel compelled to take sides or to make decisions in every situation that arises in the church. A judicious refusal to intervene or give opinion is often appropriate, especially if the pastor or another church member not involved in the dispute can offer a suitable alternative or person to help in resolution.

Love Drives Out Fear

Underpinning all these disciplines is John's promise that love is more powerful than fear. "In love there is no room for fear, but perfect love drives out fear, because fear implies punishment and whoever is afraid has not come to perfection in love." These words in 1 John 4 are not merely an exhortation to "hang in there; everything will work out for the best." It is also not an invitation to judge whether we have perfect love: "If my love is really perfect, I won't feel fear." Instead, these words remind us that we can rely on *God's* love. They are a promise that the love we experience in relationship with the resurrected Christ has the power to transform fear into assurance and to heal those wounded places that keep our ministry small and tentative. John tells us that fear is about condemnation; often, it is less the condemnation we receive from others that destroys us than the condemnation that we place on ourselves. The ministry of encouragement, with its emphasis on possibility and grace present through the Spirit, allows us to experience God's love— in our own prayers and the prayers of others, in the honesty and acceptance of friends and colleagues, and in the many ways Christ forgives and sustains us in day-to-day living. Sustained by love, we understand that life does not have to be constricted by condemnation and fear. Life is affirmed and enriched by the richness and healing we find in God's community. Life is about salvation.

Reflections

1. What factors in ministry cause you anxiety or fear?

- How do you prepare to face change?
- How do you prepare to accept and work through conflict?
- How do you prepare to admit and deal with mistakes you have made with people or in ministry?
- How do you enable yourself to share control of meetings and ministry?
- When have you admitted to your own weakness or fear? Share an example. When have you found it difficult to do so? Share an example.

2. How do you pray?

- What resources are helpful to you in your devotional life?
- What prayer support do you have from others?
- To whom could you turn to establish such prayer support?

3. Who offers you support in your ministry?

- How have you developed a collegial group where you can share honestly? If you have not yet developed such a group, how can you take steps to do so?
- Who in your congregation could be a confidential and compassionate listener for you?
- How are the people in these support groups helpful in suggesting or helping you find alternatives in "either/or" situations?

FIVE

Standing against Failure

The Ministry of Reconciliation

Barnabas suggested taking John Mark, but Paul was not in fa-
vor of taking along the man who had deserted them in Pamphylia
and had refused to share in their work. There was sharp dis-
agreement so that they parted company, and Barnabas sailed off
with Mark to Cyprus.—Acts 15:37-39

IT HAPPENS SO QUICKLY AND LUKE takes so little notice that we
just might miss it on first reading: "Paul and his companions
went by sea from Paphos to Perga in Pamphylia where John left
them to go back to Jerusalem" (Acts 13:13). When Barnabas
and Saul left for their first mission to Cyprus, John Mark accompanied them. John Mark was a young Christian who returned to Antioch with Barnabas and Paul after they had
delivered Antioch's offering to the church in Jerusalem. In Cyprus
he assisted them in their mission (Acts 13:3) and was there as
they encountered the proconsul, Sergius Paulus, and Elymas
the magician. He witnessed Paul's emergence as the main spokes-
man for the mission, and he continued with the two older men
as they sailed to the mainland and landed in Pamphylia. At this

point, John Mark suddenly left the journey and returned to Jerusalem.

Not for the first nor the last time in his narrative, Luke remains mute on details we would find helpful, or at least interesting. Why did John Mark leave the mission? His desertion followed a sea passage, a mode of travel that involved considerable danger in that time. Did John Mark suffer a loss of nerve? We know he was responsible for his mother's welfare. Did a change in family circumstance pull him back to Jerusalem? Was the transition in leadership between Paul and Barnabas a factor? The personalities of the two men involved were certainly different. Barnabas was the "son of encouragement," while we know that Paul was more confrontational and prickly. Or was this a case in which enthusiasm had brought someone to a ministry that proved to require more preparation and experience than John Mark had?

Whatever the reason for John Mark's departure, Paul was not prepared to forgive or forget. He clearly believed that the younger man had deserted him and Barnabas and that this desertion disqualified John Mark from further mission in Christ's name. There was "sharp disagreement" between Paul and Barnabas, and, again, we wish Luke had given us more detail. Why was Barnabas so sure that John Mark was now ready and Paul so certain that he was not? Had personal differences grown between Paul and Barnabas to the point that this disagreement simply provided the occasion for ending a partnership already growing sour? Luke's omission of reasons leaves us to speculate. What is clear is that their shared mission split when Paul refused to include John Mark in their new work. Paul chose Silas to accompany him to Syria and Cilicia, visiting churches he and Barnabas had previously planted and helping them continue in spiritual growth. Barnabas and John Mark left for Cyprus, presumably on a similar task.

It may seem ironic to us that Paul was so dead set against allowing the young John Mark a second chance, given his own history. When he was Saul the Pharisee rather than Paul the missionary, he had been the scourge of Christ's infant church. With the possible exception of Herod, no single individual created such fear in those who followed Christ as did Saul. Yet Christ forgave him and called him. The church—with a vital assist from Barnabas—accepted Paul and commissioned him to its ministry. He became one of its foremost leaders. As his letters show, Paul was aware how much Jesus forgave in calling him. Yet he held the past against John Mark and refused to work with him. He was even willing to end his partnership with Barnabas rather than to associate with this unreliable boy.

Possibly Paul's grudge against John Mark was intensified by the timing of the younger man's desertion. When Saul raged against the church, he was convinced that his enemies were perverting the true faith of Abraham, Isaac, Jacob, and Moses. Once confronted with God's new truth, though, he never hesitated to follow Christ or to share the gospel. John Mark claimed to be a person of faith who already had formed a relationship with Christ. Perhaps in Paul's understanding of commitment, Mark had no excuse, be it loss of nerve or mixed priorities, for pulling back from the task of discipleship once he had accepted it. While this attitude may seem more unforgiving than people who have experienced grace might find appropriate, we shall see that Paul reflects a standard many hold in today's church. Since we do not fully understand Paul's motives, we should not judge him too harshly ourselves, but it seems safe to say that his rejection of John Mark and the subsequent break with Barnabas were not Paul's finest moments.

This is not the end of the story, though. Late in his ministry, arrested again, brought to trial and awaiting his sentence, Paul wrote to his protégé Timothy: "Make every effort to come and see me as soon as you can. As it is, Demas has deserted me for love of this life and gone to Thessalonica, Crescens has gone to Galatia and Titus to Dalmatia; only Luke is with me. Bring Mark with you; I find him a useful helper in my work" (2 Tim. 4:9-11). Abandoned by some of his followers and with others called elsewhere by pastoral work, Paul asked that John Mark be sent to him. The young man he had rejected several years earlier became a valued coworker. Barnabas' instincts were correct; John Mark's usefulness to Christ was not ended by a single moment of failure, regardless of its motivation or its effect on his fellow missionaries. And Barnabas' willingness to give John Mark another opportunity to serve led to a further opportunity for reconciliation. Mark and Paul overcame their differences and were able to work together effectively.[1]

Of course, the stories of Saul's transformation and of John Mark's growth as a disciple are not the only accounts in Scripture of someone given a second chance. The other giant of the early church, Peter, is remembered vividly for his failure and his forgiveness. Every year during the seasons of Lent and Easter, we are reminded of Peter's boast, "Lord, I will never leave you," and of Jesus' prediction of betrayal and denial. Three times Peter fearfully denied that he knew this Galilean on trial before the high priest and Pilate. At the cock's crow, he was reminded that Jesus knew him better than he knew himself. He failed Jesus at his master's hour of greatest need. Only a few days later, along the shore of the sea he had fished so many times, Peter was blessed by forgiveness and given an instruction, "Feed my sheep." He received a second chance to love and serve in the name of his master. Then, after the Council of Jerusalem, Peter came under the influence of those who still regarded Gentile Christians as unclean and refused to dine with them. Only after Paul called him to account did Peter remember the lesson taught him in Joppa: "What I have made clean, you must not call unclean." (This sometimes overlooked story, which reminds us how difficult it was for Jewish Christians to accept the Gentiles fully, is told in Galatians 2:11-14.) Once again, Peter responded to the challenge to love fully. He died bringing the gospel to pagan Rome.

An unfortunate tendency persists within the church, even today, to divide God into two personalities. According to this scheme, the Old Testament portrays a "God of wrath" and the New a "God of grace" or a "God of love." It is true that Hebrew Scripture can stun us with scenes of graphic violence and threats of punishment that are attributed to God. (For that matter, so can Revelation.) But the Old Testament is also filled with other pictures of God. Scripture begins with God calling a world out of chaos; God is a loving, even playful, Creator. God creates a nation from a motley tribe of Egyptian slaves in the exodus and recreates that nation after their exile. Story after story tells us of God's yearning to heal and forgive and God's commitment to reconciliation with those who have betrayed and disappointed him. This commitment is extended past the nation to individuals. David received a second chance after his adultery with Bathsheba and the murder of Uriah, even though he did not escape the consequences of his actions. Jonah is allowed to take up the mission to Nineveh he tried to avoid and is forgiven when he rebels against his own success. Even Sodom and Gomorrah are offered the possibility of multiple chances in the bargaining session between Abraham and God that precedes the cities' destruction. After generations of faithlessness followed by forgiveness finally eventuate in Israel's destruction, the seeds for renewal and return are planted in the faithful remnant who hear and obey the words of the prophets of the Exile. Despite our nearsightedness to this scriptural reality, God is consistently committed to offering us the possibility of reconciliation, the second chance. Barnabas has good precedent for his willingness to work with John Mark.

The Church and Failure

Given this wealth of scriptural witness, it is discouraging that pastors and congregations can so often be blind to the power of second chances and reconciliation and to God's mandate that we offer second chances to others. We especially find it difficult to forgive and respond in a healing manner to the mistakes and failures of other Christians. Indeed, the failure of the faithful is often met not with understanding and compassion but with self-righteousness and rejection. A husband or wife who succumbs to the temptation of an extramarital relationship, a recovering alcoholic who slips off the wagon, an overextended bank manager who is discovered "borrowing" from a trust fund can pretty quickly find a congregation an inhospitable and unforgiving family. (As I relate below, my experience leads me to understand alcoholism and other addictions as disease, not sin. My experience also suggests that some church people either reject this understanding altogether or find it easy to accept until the disease becomes active in the life of a fellow Christian.) Lapses in ethical or moral decisions are serious, of course, and they need to be acknowledged and opened to the healing power of repentance. Still, too many congregations rush to judge and condemn. Such condemnation makes it difficult, if not impossible, for a sinner to obtain reconciliation and healing from sin within the church, the very community that was created to offer the good news of repentance and forgiveness. Such distortion of the church's mission serves to validate the image of pompous hypocrisy that popular culture often pins on Christians.

It is not only such serious lapses in behavior that lead Christians to judgment and condemnation of others. Just as John Mark's return to Jerusalem seems less grave to us than Paul's response might indicate, relatively minor mistakes by pastors and laypeople engaged in ministry can result in severe criticism and outright censure. Second chances can be hard to come by in some congregations. Ask the pastor who loses her temper with the wrong people present at a meeting, or the stewardship chairman who oversees a disastrous financial campaign. A few years ago, I served near a congregation that asked its volunteer youth leader to resign. He had invited the youth to a Halloween party rather than providing a Christian alternative and had even showed Vincent Price horror films in the process. Because he had encouraged "satanic activity," he was not allowed to explain or apologize, but merely to resign. The same lack of second chances can be true within denominational structures. Pastors who fail to succeed in a congregation where success is expected or who ignite conflict within a congregation through a lapse of judgment often feel that they are tainted for the rest of their ministry by this single experience—a feeling that is often accurate.

Each church that I have served as pastor, as well as the one in which I grew up, has included members who see reconciliation and forgiveness—the offering of a second chance—as mere sentimentality. Much as Paul acted toward Mark, they approach the sins of others with a "one strike and you're out" attitude. I will deal more with this attitude in the next section, but it is important for us to recognize its effects. Many people who might otherwise be open to a relationship with Christ are turned away by the attitudes they see and the treatment they receive from Christians. To proclaim the reality and power of love and forgiveness and then to treat each other or those outside the church with a lack of either is simply destructive of our efforts at evangelism. Again, the greatest obstacle to Christ is often Christians.

Against this attitude of judgment and self-righteousness, Barnabas offers a model of true reconciliation. His willingness to invest time and instruction in John Mark, despite Paul's rejection of the young man, calls us to make a similar commitment to those who have "failed." Offering reconciliation and a second chance is vital to the church's character and mission. When we succeed at reconciliation, we have demonstrated the love of Christ and have taken an important step in our mission to make disciples. When we let arrogance and judgmental attitudes interfere with forgiveness and healing, we have failed in our mission, we have failed Christ, and we have failed ourselves.

Our discussion so far has attempted to explain how the absence of reconciliation warps our mission and fails Christ. The last failure mentioned, failing ourselves, may be less clear. Remembering Jesus' teachings on forgiveness may make that failure more clear. The Lord's Prayer makes a direct connection. We are instructed to ask God for the same grace we have extended toward others; "forgive us our trespasses *as we forgive those who trespass against us*." The parable of the unforgiving debtor found in Matthew 18:23-35 broadens the picture of one who claims grace but refuses to share it. Unwilling to extend grace to one who owes him far less than he owes his forgiving master, the servant is called to account for his lack of mercy and held responsible for the debts he had been forgiven. In the same way, our lack of grace and forgiveness toward others binds us more closely to the results of our own mistakes and imperfections.

Reconciliation and Response

I noted above that we are often accused of sentimentality when we offer others a second chance. Properly understood, though, reconciliation has very little to do with sentiment. In Scripture, reconciliation is always paired with challenge and growth. Saul's reconciliation with the Christ he had attacked demanded that he reorient his entire life. As noted in the previous chapter, this reorientation required Saul to struggle with his own past and with the requirements of a new life (Philippians 3). This new life called him to face and accept the judgment of those whom he had terrorized (Acts 9:26-27). Peter, too, found that the forgiveness he was offered was linked to service to Christ. In essence, Jesus told Peter (John 21:15-19), "You are forgiven. Despite your denial, I continue to love you and accept you as my disciple. Now how will you respond?" Feeding Christ's sheep—the challenge Jesus offered along with forgiveness—transformed Peter. The disciple who cowered in the high priest's courtyard became the one who challenged the court of the Sanhedrin in the name of his Master a few short weeks later.

When Barnabas chose to mentor John Mark, we would expect that he offered the guidance and companionship that he had once shared with Saul; but these did not come without cost. Mark would be called to share in the joys, challenges, and struggles that the young man had avoided in the earlier trip. The second chance of Scripture is complete grace, which is to say love and forgiveness offered freely and without reservation; but God's grace always comes with the possibility and necessity for spiritual growth. Grace initiates the opportunity for learning the deeper responsibilities of discipleship.

Healing through Reconciliation

Perhaps a personal illustration can make clear how transforming reconciliation can be. For the first 12 years of my ministry, I drank alcohol daily and often excessively. It is difficult to pinpoint the exact moment when my drinking became self-destructive, but since I tended to be a stress drinker, this stage was probably reached early on, perhaps even before I began serving my first church. Both alcohol and the abuse of it accompanied me through my first two appointments. By God's grace, these two congregations remember me as a good pastor, though I am certain my problem was noticed, and I know my drinking harmed my effectiveness as a pastor.

It was a parishioner who finally forced me to confront my addiction. She had credibility, not least because of her own recovery from alcohol and drug abuse, and I trusted her. She spoke with compassion but also with the clear message that I needed to quit drinking and to do so immediately. Her willingness to risk our friendship to speak the truth opened my heart. I was being given the chance to change before my ministry, my marriage, and my health were damaged beyond recovery. At that time, I was preparing for a move to a new congregation. It is unlikely that I could have survived that move without confronting my alcohol abuse, and, given the injuries already suffered by the new congregation because of conflict with its previous pastor, it is unlikely that parishioners could have avoided the further damage that I would undoubtedly have inflicted. With a supportive network of friends and colleagues, I have found other ways of managing stress and fear; both my ministry and my relationship with God have deepened. Had I been met with judgment rather than the compassion and forgiveness Christ brought me through my friends, colleagues, and members of that congregation, I would likely be out of the ordained ministry today.

Although I have used the term "second chance" in this chapter, reconciliation will often require more than one attempt. I have a friend who serves a congregation in an urban setting. One of her parishioners is a former pastor who was removed from the ordained ministry for pastoral incompetence. In his 14 years as a pastor, Terry served in 11 churches. The problem was not his preaching or administrative skills. He simply did not like and could not or would not carry out pastoral calling. Terry had been up-front about his intent to take his gifts into a specialized ministry outside the parish, but it had also been made clear to him that this step could not be taken until he had a successful period of parish ministry. The mutual inflexibility of the cabinet (no specialized ministry without a record of success in parish work) and of Terry (refusing offers to help him gain skills in pastoral care and calling) led to many short, unhappy appointments and the eventual decision to recall Terry's credentials as an ordained pastor.

When my friend arrived at the church Terry attended, she discovered that his passion for Christian service was intact. At her invitation, Terry preached when she was away. She discovered that he enjoyed teaching and was more than happy to help begin an adult class. He became involved with an outreach program to Hispanics in the neighborhood; he was an asset to the pastor leading the program. After years of struggling and being labeled a failure, Terry has found a new vocation in that local church. It is not the ministry he envisioned, but it makes use of his gifts and affords benefits to a struggling church. Terry is no longer a failure to himself or to those who know him; he has returned to ministry for Christ.

Could Terry have found his ministry outside the institutional church? Probably, although Terry's family history—his grandfather and two uncles had served as pastors—led him to see ordained ministry as his true calling. Others who have felt alienated from or rejected by local congregations have found ways to serve Christ in other settings. I have colleagues who have left or have been removed from congregational ministry and then found a new call in teaching, nursing-home administration, full-time evangelism, music ministry, or writing, for example. While most of these have maintained their credentials of ordination, some have taken early retirement or stepped out of the pastorate altogether. Many miss the seasonal rituals and the daily contact with congregational life—although certainly not all do—but still find that they are fulfilling God's call in their new ministry.

It is not only pastors who need or find a second chance at ministry in the world beyond the church walls. I met Steven on an Emmaus Walk where he was serving as a group leader.[2] Steven had felt that he was a failure in his local congregation. Recruited to be a church-school teacher, he had been unable to hold the attention of his third- and fourth-grade class. He felt a call to work with youth but couldn't relate to the program offered, or to the youth leaders ("They made me feel old and out of it"). His pastor was sympathetic and suggested the Emmaus Walk as a way to explore his call. Steven was a successful businessman active in Rotary. Emmaus helped him to discern that he was called to ministry through this community organization. He began with an invitation to other leaders in the neighborhood where his business was located to meet weekly for prayer and Bible study. Out of these morning prayer and study sessions, Steven discovered a number of colleagues with a heart for helping community youth. This shared concern and a contact within the school system led to the establishment of a mentoring program that connects Christian adults with "at-risk" youth from the elementary and middle schools closest to the downtown area served by the businesses. This program, in turn, led to a partnership between the suburban church where Steven worships and a church in the schools' neighborhood. Together, they supply funds and volunteers for tutoring and recreational programs that take place in that urban congregation. Although his ministry has affected his congregation and its vision, Steven's focus remains on the community youth, his collegial prayer and Bible study, and Emmaus. Steven's story is duplicated in many settings and multiple forms of ministry. Local congregations and pastors may fail laypeople like Steven through our inability to help them discover a ministry outside congregational programs or to recognize such a ministry as a fulfillment of their call from God.

One of the most recognized and quoted verses of Scripture is John 3:16: "For this is how God loved the world: he gave his only Son, so that everyone who believes in him may not perish but may have eternal life." It seems to me that when we stop there, we have only half the thought. The message is completed by the verse that follows: "For God sent his Son into the world not to judge [condemn] the world, but so that through him the world might be saved" (John 3:17). The point of God's action in Christ is not to punish the unfaithful, the sinful, the ignorant, and the willful. The point of God's action in Christ is that all these, as well as all those of us who manage to be intermittently faithful in our discipleship, are meant for reconciliation. We all receive multiple second chances—even after we recognize that we have been saved. Whenever we deny this chance for reconciliation to others through a refusal to forgive or by condemning or writing them off after a single "failure" or set of failures, we deny the true gift of Jesus' death and resurrection. To offer second chances "seventy times seven" (and to recognize our own need for them) is the work of ministry.

Reflections

1. In what ways have you received "second chances" or experienced reconciliation in your personal life? In what ways have you experienced them in your ministry?

   • Who was your Barnabas? That is, who gave you encouragement and helped hold you accountable during your second chance?

2. In what ways have you been called to offer "second chances" or reconciliation to others during your ministry?

   • What was the cost to you? How did you offer encouragement?

SIX

Authenticity in Ministry

Character and Call

There was a Levite of Cypriot origin called Joseph, whom the apostles surnamed Barnabas (which means "son of encouragement"). He owned a piece of land and he sold it and brought the money and presented it to the apostles.—Acts 4:36-37

There [Barnabas] was glad to see for himself that God had given grace, and he urged them all to remain faithful to the Lord with heartfelt devotion, for he was a good man, filled with the Holy Spirit and with faith. And a large number of people were won over to the Lord.—Acts 11:23-24

IN HIS ENTIRE SERVICE TO CHRIST, perhaps the single most important task of encouragement undertaken by Barnabas was his sponsorship of Saul of Tarsus. As we have seen earlier, Barnabas' intervention was needed to persuade a suspicious and fearful group of apostles that Saul had truly been changed through his personal encounter with Christ. The apostles responded to Barnabas because they had experience with him that gave them confidence in his character. They trusted his judgment. The level of trust the church had in Barnabas was such that it overcame the level of mistrust the apostles had for Saul, which was, of course, quite deep. What was evident in Barnabas' character that allowed this trust to form? Quite simply, it was the quality we call *authenticity.* Barnabas had allowed his own life to be shaped by God's call. When he called others to follow Christ, he did so as one who was faithful in his own response. We see this fidelity in his initial appearance in Luke's narrative. At a time when the church was trying to find means to support its ministry and its poorest members, Barnabas—already known as and given the name of an encourager—sold a piece of land and gave the proceeds to be used as the apostles chose.

The second passage noted above describes the congregational response to Barnabas' ministry in Antioch. He encouraged the new Christians of that city to remain true to Christ "with heartfelt devotion," or as the New International Version (NIV) puts it, "with all their hearts" (Acts 11:33). His encouragement mattered to these new Christians, for they experienced Barnabas and his faith as genuine, as the apostles had before them. He is described as "good" and "filled with the Holy Spirit and with faith." As we would probably say of those individuals who led us to faith, Barnabas was a living advertisement for the faith he taught and preached. The integrity of Barnabas' life and his attentiveness to God's call demonstrated the truth of his faith.

Notice that authenticity has two components. Obviously, Barnabas brought certain personal qualities to his ministry of encouragement. In an earlier chapter, we identified four such qualities that are indispensable to the ministry of encouragement: humility, the ability to deal with conflict, vulnerability, and integrity. But Barnabas' authenticity went beyond these personal qualities; Barnabas was also authentic in his response to God's call. Barnabas' call was perhaps not as explicit as Saul's experience on the Damascus road or Peter's rooftop experience in Joppa, but his call to the ministry of encouragement was as authentic. When he sold his land and gave the money to the apostles, Barnabas was showing generosity, but he was also responding to God's call to care for the poor. When he stood by Saul and John Mark and affirmed their discipleship, he was displaying the qualities of patience and hope; he was also heeding God's call for reconciliation (and perhaps reaffirming for Saul and John Mark that God was truly calling them to ministry). Barnabas' call is most explicit in Luke's narration of Barnabas' and Saul's extension of their mission from Antioch to Cyprus and beyond. Here, both responded to the leading of the Holy Spirit as it came through the call of the congregation in Antioch.

In Scripture, authenticity is variously called "faithfulness," "seeking the Lord," "walking in the ways of the Lord," and "righteousness." Each of these words describes a relationship with God as much as it describes a personal quality or combination of qualities. When we seek pastors or leaders within the laity, we often focus on the personal gifts the potential leader brings. But in Scripture, people are chosen less for talents we might find important or for a high "success" rate in previous ministry than for their attentiveness to God's call and fidelity to God's leading.

The ministry of Moses provides one example of such attentiveness and fidelity. The efforts of Cecil B. DeMille and other filmmakers have convinced many of us that Moses was a mighty worker for God who overcame Pharaoh and led the Hebrew people to freedom through sheer force of personality. The narratives of Exodus and Numbers give us a different picture. Although Moses could often be a powerful commander and did possess that elusive quality we call charisma, these traits are not overemphasized in Scripture. Moses is not chosen because he possesses such gifts; indeed, he appears timid rather than commanding at the moment of his call (Exodus 3-4). "Who am I that I should go?" he asks. When God persists in that choice, Moses reminds God of his (Moses') lack of credibility with the

Hebrew people. When God provides him with the various signs to establish needed credibility, Moses pleads a lack of eloquence. God agrees to allow Aaron to be Moses' designated speaker. With all his objections answered, Moses simply begs off: "Lord, let someone else do this."

Moses is chosen despite his reluctance and perceived lack of persuasive abilities, because he will learn to follow God's instruction. Moses' authenticity as a leader derives from his ability to hear God and his obedience to God's call. Moses certainly grows into a powerful leader. He will plead for his people before God; he will also complain about their lack of faith and grow weary of their complaints against him and against God. But he has the ability to advocate for them at times and to discipline them at others because he remains centered on God's authority and guidance. When Moses loses this attentiveness at Meribah, he plays God, altering God's instruction and claiming credit with God ("Must *we* bring you water out of this rock?") for providing a miraculous flow of water (Num. 20:1-13). As a consequence of this lapse, God bars Moses from entering the Promised Land with the people he led for so long.

Authenticity and Speaking for God

The issue of authenticity or its absence often arises in Scripture around the question of false prophets and false teaching: How can we tell who speaks for God and who does not? At the simplest level, the difference between false prophet and faithful is the faithful prophet's willingness to speak God's word even when it hurts or when others do not wish to hear. False prophets prefer to give words of encouragement even when such encouragement is false. They cry peace when there is none. True prophets are also more often willing to see the complexity of a situation, to understand that easy answers are rare.

In the book of Jeremiah, the conflict between true prophet and false arises in the context of Jeremiah's warning against false prophets (Jer. 23:9-32) and through a confrontation between Jeremiah and Hananiah, one of the royal prophets (Jer. 28:1-17). Jeremiah steadfastly avoids cheap grace and ties the prospect of Israel's salvation to repentance. In contrast, Hananiah preaches hope when the time for hope in deliverance from Babylon is past and the time has arrived for repentance and acceptance of God's discipline. Jeremiah denounces this false hope and, although his words are rejected, is proved correct. Jeremiah pays a price for his authenticity, of course. In a poignant series of passages, Jeremiah reminds God of the cost of his obedience and complains that God has often left him hanging despite his faithful service. Not many of us will pay so high a cost as Jeremiah, but it is clear that authenticity is not a guarantee of trouble-free ministry or a comfortable life.[1]

The prophet Ezekiel deals with false leadership in another context: shepherds who care for themselves rather than for their sheep (Ezekiel 34). While it is true that Israel's religious leaders played a political function that is not usually a component of the contemporary pastor's role, the main point still holds. The welfare of the flock is primary, not the comfort of the shepherd. To see a congregation or other pastoral assignment as the means to an end for my own agenda or advancement is to mishear and distort God's call to me as pastor. Nor does the metaphor of pastor as shepherd seem authentic if it leads me as pastor to see the congregation as a flock dependent on me rather than on God, unable to find direction or nourishment without my firm hand leading them. The role of pastor is not one of directing a congregation as the cast of a movie or play is directed. Instead, as we have seen in chapter 2, the pastor is called to work in partnership with laity to deepen and widen the ministry of the whole church.

Certainly, pastors are not alone in this difficulty. Lay leaders may also allow their own agendas to preempt authentic response to God's call. Although, as I stated earlier, pastors can exaggerate this tendency out of their own motives, tradition can exert a strong pull on lay leadership. The reasons are not difficult to understand; church traditions are formed through a congregation's experience and are very much a part of congregational identity. Remember Bea's worry (see chapter 4), that in accepting congregational change, she might lose the sense of family that can bind a congregation together. Traditions become traditions because they have been effective or have brought meaning to a community. It is when traditions maintain importance as they lose effectiveness, or as they block the action of a Spirit that "makes all things new," that they can become dangerous and debilitating to a congregation's ministry.

Lay leaders may lose their focus on God's call in other ways. Some, like Moses at his moment of call, have been chosen for leadership positions but still underrate their own gifts and possibilities for ministry. Or they underrate the possibilities for the congregations they lead:

"I'm too old."

"We have too much to do already."

"I can't ————. I don't know how."

"That's the pastor's job."

"We just don't have enough volunteers."

At times I have heard all these words from people at First Church, several of whom have overcome their lack of confidence and are now leading ministries. Guiding a leadership team or an entire congregation through an inventory of spiritual gifts may help overcome this block, but it is sometimes difficult to overcome lay leaders' and other members' reluctance to do such a study. There is a flip side to the problem of undervaluing our worth; some lay leaders guard their role or position jealously, from the pastor and other laity alike. They may see themselves as the only ones capable of doing or continuing the ministry effectively, and they may wish to keep things that way, refusing to help train others or to share the opportunities and responsibilities that come with the position. The idea simply does not register that God may call a church member to step out of a role to try something new or to make way for another to discover a ministry.

In all these cases—those who elevate tradition as their highest value, those who underrate their own possibilities, and those who overrate their own importance—the pastor and other lay leaders need to pray for the best way to open them to new possibilities and to call them into the process of prayer and discernment. Especially in the first and last cases, there may be a need for caring confrontation and conflict; it will be to everyone's benefit if this is done only after an adequate period of preparation, consisting of prayer for the Spirit's guidance through the process of confrontation and for healthy resolution.

Temptation and Authenticity

The greatest hindrance to our authentic response to God's call may come in the form of temptation—the desires and drive for self-fulfillment contained in every human life. The temptations of Jesus are a direct challenge to the authenticity of his ministry (Luke 4:1-13). In the wilderness, Satan's tests are designed to draw Jesus' attention to his own possibilities for power and away from God's call.

"Turn these stones to bread and satisfy your hunger."

"Cast yourself down; surely God will send angels to protect you."

"The kingdoms of the world are yours if you only worship me."

Satan promises the rewards of the world if Jesus will turn to the world's values. But Jesus remains centered on God's word and God's purpose. So Satan leaves "until an opportune moment." What this last phrase suggests is that Jesus did not pass a set of tests in the wilderness and conquer temptation once and for all. He was tempted as we are, which is to say continually and with great variety. It is in this context that the words of the Letter to the Hebrews speak to me: "For the high priest we have is not incapable of feeling our weaknesses with us, but has been put to the test in exactly the same way as ourselves, apart from sin" (Heb. 4:15).

Perhaps Jesus was sometimes tempted by his own popularity and success, as we all can be. Perhaps he longed to live a less complicated, less conflicted life. Perhaps Jesus was tempted by the expectations of the crowd, as we can be tempted by the projections and hopes of the congregations in which we work and share ministry. Perhaps he was tempted in relationship with the women who cared for him and who had found an acceptance in Jesus they had found in no other man, as we can be tempted by the physical attractions and emotional needs of those with whom we work. Although Jesus did not have to deal with the false urgency that plagues so many schedules in our culture of busy-ness, proper use of time may have been an issue for him, too; it is suggested in Mark's version of the feeding of the 5,000 (Mark 6:30-44) that Jesus sometimes found it difficult to take needed time aside for prayer, solitude, and renewal when he saw the tremendous needs of those who flocked to him. The yearning of the crowd for spectacle may have tempted Jesus to use his miraculous powers to focus attention upon himself, as Moses did at Meribah, and he was certainly tempted in Gethsemane by fear and physical dread. Although not based directly in Scripture, the temptation Nikos Kazantzakis imagines in his novel *The Last Temptation of Christ*—the temptation to live a quiet, ordinary life as a Palestinian carpenter—might truly have been a struggle for Jesus. Jesus is a model for authentic ministry not because he was immune to the temptations we face but because he experienced the same struggles we do.

Attentiveness to God

The ministry of encouragement is convincing only if the encourager is authentic. Unless we keep the need for authenticity primary among our daily concerns, we run the risk of losing track of who we are and what we are about as Christians. We are faced by many matters of real significance and by too many matters masquerading as significant for us to neglect the discipline of listening for God's guidance. Attentiveness to God is our guide through the conflicting demands and false urgencies of our lives and is absolutely necessary if we are to keep faith with our own gifts and ministry and encourage others to do the same.

In *Working the Angles,* Eugene Peterson points to the result of inadequate attention to pastoral authenticity with a vivid metaphor.

> The pastors of America have metamorphosed into a company of shopkeepers, and the shops they keep are churches. . . . Some of them are very good shopkeepers. They attract a lot of customers, pull in great sums of money, develop splendid reputations. Yet it is still shopkeeping; religious shopkeeping, to be sure, but shopkeeping all the same. The marketing strategies of the fast-food franchise occupy the waking minds of these entrepreneurs.[2]

Peterson's use of the term "shopkeeping" is strong language; nonetheless, I believe it is an apt description of what happens to our ministries when we become excessively concerned with measurable success. Numbers matter if they represent people the church is calling into discipleship and relationship with Christ. As soon as numbers become the measure of a "successful" ministry, we have made people objects to be accumulated rather than souls to be fed, and our ministry becomes idolatrous rather than authentic. Strong language—but the reality is that success remains a seductive temptation for us all, and denominational policies and attitudes are too often more likely to pander to this seduction than to help pastors resist it.

Peterson continues:

> The biblical fact is that there are no successful churches. There are, instead, communities of sinners, gathered before God week after week in towns and villages all over the world. The Holy Spirit gathers them and does his work in them. . . . The pastor's responsibility is to keep the community attentive to God. It is this responsibility that is being abandoned in spades.[3]

As we have seen, Moses, Jeremiah, and Barnabas relied on attentiveness to God as the foundation for their ministries. Clergy are certainly not the only church leaders who have this responsibility. Both clergy and lay leaders must ourselves be attentive to God, and we share the responsibility to help others understand what attentiveness to God means and requires. The second of these can be accomplished only if we are faithful to the first.

Pastors are often troubled by another issue that is candidly expressed in the confessions of Jeremiah. What happens when the role of pastor is at odds with the hopes and needs of the person called to the role? The congregations we serve have expectations for the role of pastor, though these expectations can differ greatly from congregation to congregation and from member to member. Such expectations often reflect each congregation's history with its pastors. Many congregations are used to having a "pastor-in-charge," working under what I call the CEO model of ordained ministry. Some congregations have had a series of conflicts with pastors or have been betrayed by their pastors—not just through the sexual misconduct that has grabbed headlines in recent years, but betrayals through violations of confidentiality, deliberate formation and manipulation of cliques, financial abuses, and abrupt departure for "greener pastures." With such a wide variety of expectations for the pastor, those of us who are ordained often feel stretched beyond our own recognition. Is there a real "me" inside the pastor? We complicate matters by carrying our own images of who a pastor is and how a pastor should act, which may or may not fit our idea of who we are or how we wish to act. This image is formed in the church where we were brought to faith, though it is also altered by our experiences as pastors, both good and bad. My conversations with fellow pastors indicate that this conflict between the role and the person is complicated by the changing role of the church and of clergy in a culture that is less inclined to offer automatic respect or even to find relevance in either.

I know of pastors who wrestle with these issues of identity their entire careers As noted in chapter 4, failure to resolve them can lead clergy to create and don masks. Some leave or are removed from ordained ministry when the issues cannot be resolved. But I do believe that resolution to the conflict between the pastoral role and personal needs can be found if we keep our attentiveness to remaining authentic before God.[4] Even a casual reading of Scripture reveals that God does not choose a single personality type to do his work. Moses was fully Moses, Jeremiah fully Jeremiah, Lydia fully Lydia, and Barnabas fully Barnabas as they followed God's calling, and no one would mistake one of these individuals for another. God calls women and men of differing gifts and personalities to carry out ministry, all sinners and all flawed vessels. We are called to be who we are, not to fulfill some generic model of a pastor. Whether clergy or laity, we are called to give ourselves to God, not to lose our identities but to become fully ourselves through following him.

A different kind of identity conflict, experienced by laity, also requires attention to God's call. Both pastors and lay leaders often make the mistake of assuming that Christian vocation is found and fulfilled only through congregational ministries. Two factors in this assumption are the tendency to pay more attention to the recruitment of people to help with congregational ministries than to recognize and affirm other forms of ministry, and the perception that congregational work is somehow more holy than work "in the world." This kind of tunnel vision neglects the fact that most laypeople will find very real and crucial opportunities for ministry in their daily activities and contacts with others—in their families, jobs, schools, and other community organizations. These opportunities may be the true calling of our laypeople, not to the exclusion of congregational ministries but as a further extension of Christ's word and work. If they are to be authentic in their ministry and the church is to be faithful to its call to make disciples, it is vital for us both to affirm people in these ministries—not load them with guilt because they are not available for yet another committee assignment—and to help them gain the skills needed for being disciples in nonchurch settings.

The Search for Authenticity

How do we pursue God's answers to our questions about authenticity? The pursuit may seem disappointingly basic to some readers, and therefore unsatisfying. There is no substitute for prayer, immersion in Scripture, and mutual accountability with one or more colleagues who also seek to be faithful to God's call. Lengthy elaboration on these disciplines is beyond the scope of this book. Besides, wonderful resources are available to help the seeker for the Spirit. Eugene Peterson, Richard Foster, and Terry Tekyl are just three authors whose works have benefited me greatly. What I can offer is something in the way of a negative witness. Those periods in my life as pastor when I have been neglectful of or inattentive to these disciplines are precisely the times when I have also been inattentive to my ministry and neglectful of people who deserved my love and attention. The disciplines of prayer, Scripture, and mutual accountability are not assurance against mistake or failure, but they certainly reduce the risk and also prepare us for repentance in its scriptural sense—turning toward positive change as well as away from destructive behavior or habits.

These disciplines will have their greatest influence on our ministry when they become the daily substance of our walk with God. When we ignore them or allow them to be displaced by other, "more pressing" pastoral duties or personal commitments, whatever success or progress we have achieved as pastors and as persons will prove transitory. We should take as a warning to us the number of "successful" pastorates brought down by burnout, by the betrayals noted earlier, by drug abuse, and by weary ministry routines of "going through the motions" on the way to retirement. All these are symptoms of the same inner hollowness.

Encouragement and Authenticity

The ministry of encouragement as described in the previous chapters is not just another strategy, program, or technique for ministry. Barnabas' ministry did not follow a neat 12-step process to success. It should go without saying that, as leaders, we do not pretend to be encouraging as a way to manipulate our congregations into following our own predetermined goals. Rather than manipulating the members or following someone else's recipe for success, we are led by the ministry of encouragement to

seek the guidance of the Spirit through prayer, Scripture reading, and mutual accountability. The reason we seek authenticity
is that it is essential to the Christian's faithful ministry, to fulfilling Jesus' final commandment: "Go, therefore, and make disciples of all nations" (Matt. 28:19).

We discovered during our process of discernment at First
Church that one of the most powerful guides for discerning
God's call to us is communal prayer. As we teach and talk of
prayer, many pastors and lay leaders alike overemphasize the
need for individual prayer, possibly as a logical consequence of
the Protestant and evangelical emphasis on individual salvation.
We forget that we are saved *as individuals* but saved *for community*. Salvation is, among other things, being united with a chosen people, the body of Christ with all its necessary and honored
parts. Jesus' promise about prayer emphasizes community: "In
truth I tell you once again, if two of you on earth agree to ask
anything at all, it will be granted to you by my Father in heaven.
For where two or three meet in my name, I am there among
them" (Matt. 18:19-20). Individual prayer is necessary, but the
power of prayer is deepened and multiplied by prayer in community.

Communal prayer is too important to reduce to the few
moments we share each week in our worship services. Creating
opportunities for the body of Christ to pray together for the
ministry of the church is a vital part of seeking the Spirit. Making available a variety of times for people to come together in
prayer is a helpful way to involve as many of the congregation as
have interest in participating. In our prayer gatherings at First,
we have found it helpful to have at least one specific request as a
focal point—prayer for church-school teachers, prayer for a place
to house a community prayer room, prayer for guidance in
meeting a community need for support of troubled marriages.
This helps us begin with a shared purpose. Within this guide-

line, of course, we leave both time and silence for the Spirit to inspire us and nudge us toward other prayer needs and new insights.

The ministry of encouragement requires authenticity in allowing ministry to develop through the congregation's needs, hopes, and gifts, and to do so at the Spirit's pace. Encouragement requires that we truly listen to the dreams, insights, and frustrations of the people to whom we are sent and that we refrain from molding them to fit a preconceived program for ministry, even if it has been successful elsewhere. Encouragement is not about remaking a congregation in our own image, nor does it ask a congregation to duplicate another church's success. Encouragement leads us to partnership in ministry with disciples who are already striving to follow God's call and allowing their work and its results to call others to ministry. As we encourage, we pay attention to Paul's words to the church at Corinth: "Though I am free and belong to no man, I make myself a slave to everyone, to win as many as possible. . . . I have become all things to all men so that by all possible means I might save some" (1 Cor. 9:19, 22b). Paul's attitude does not express a lack of sincerity; he is not suggesting that we be all things to all people simply to manipulate or control them. Instead, Paul encourages us to adapt ourselves to the strengths and needs of our congregations, not to expect each congregation we serve to adapt to ours.

The ministry of encouragement also allows us and challenges us to accept decisions by a congregation and its leaders with which we do not agree or about which we may have mixed feelings. When laypeople from our congregation were ready to open the Mount Sterling Community Center, I encouraged the idea as a long-term goal. When it came time to commit, though, I had second (and third and fourth) thoughts. We were signing a yearlong lease with no budget or guaranteed income and, at the time of the signing, no commitment from other churches to help with the burden. We were committing ourselves to move the food pantry from our building—one of the main community-based ministries we had. How would it look—how would *I* be perceived—if this all collapsed around us? Fortunately, God kept my mouth shut until I had time to remember who was in charge of this ministry—the Spirit had led us to this point and would continue with us if we trusted. I was able to express honest confidence in the center's future when others in the church brought up similar objections. We have had bumps in the road and, I suspect, will have more, but the center is open and has spiritual and financial support across the community. When encouragement is authentic, mutual respect and encouragement prevail between pastor and laity.

As church leaders, we are as much a product of our culture as are the congregations we serve or, for that matter, as those people who have no relationship with the church. Many of us have been trained to be skeptical of stories in which obstacles melt away, support comes from unlikely sources, and things fall into place when logic says they should not; I was a skeptic myself until I experienced the Spirit's power. Perhaps the most important truth we can learn and share with the churches we lead is that the guidance and power of the Spirit are as accessible to our congregations as they were to the men and women described in the book of Acts. If we are willing to give up attempts to control the direction of our ministries and instead seek to discern the Spirit's direction, our ministry will be both authentic and effective. No ministry will be effective in the long run unless it is rooted in discernment by both laity and pastors. We can only become Barnabas by authentically searching for God's guidance and will.

Reflections

1. In what way have you experienced God's call to discipleship?

   - How are your personal gifts and strengths being used in your ministry?
   - What difficulties or temptations do you find in remaining faithful to your call?

2. In what ways are you staying attentive to your call?

   - How do you create opportunities to remain faithful in prayer and in the reading and study of Scripture?
   - Who are the people that help support you and hold you accountable to your call?
   - How do you purposefully search for God's guidance in your life and ministry?

SEVEN

A Ministry in Process

[Those added to the church at Pentecost] remained faithful to the teaching of the apostles, to the brotherhood, to the breaking of the bread and to the prayers. And everyone was filled with awe; the apostles worked many signs and miracles. And all who shared the faith owned everything in common; they sold their goods and possessions and distributed the proceeds among themselves according to what each one needed. Each day, with one heart, they regularly went to the Temple but met in their houses for the breaking of bread; they shared their food gladly and generously; they praised God and were looked up to by everyone. Day by day the Lord added to their community those destined to be saved.—Acts 2:43-47*

[At Antioch, Barnabas] was glad to see for himself that God had given grace, and he urged [encouraged] them all to remain faithful to the Lord with heartfelt devotion; for he was a good man, filled with the Holy Spirit and with faith. And a large number of people were won over to the Lord. Barnabas then left for Tarsus to look for Saul, and when he found him he brought him to Antioch. And it happened that they stayed together in that church a whole year, instructing a large number of people. It was at Antioch that the disciples were first called "Christians."—Acts 11:23-26*

111

MORE THAN ONCE IN THESE PAGES, I have noted that the ministry of encouragement is a process that will differ from church to church and from individual to individual rather than a one-size-fits-all program. In the passages above, we see two very different responses to the presence of the encouraging Spirit. The first describes a church under the full influence of the Spirit. Signs and miracles are evident, not the least of which is the people's generosity with their property. No one goes without the necessities of life. The people worship together daily and share table fellowship and Holy Communion regularly. Their generosity and joy and thanksgiving win them admiration throughout Jerusalem and are apparently contagious; Luke tells us that more people became a part of this community daily.

The second passage describes a congregation more familiar to us. It is the picture of a church *becoming* receptive to the Spirit. The Christians at Antioch were learning what discipleship means and attempting to discern where the wind of the Spirit might be directing them. We are told that Barnabas and Saul labor with them a year, teaching them and encouraging them in their faith. During this time of maturing and growth, their neighbors begin to call them *Christians*, implying that their lives changed in a way evident to others. As noted in chapter 2, we have no details about what or how Barnabas and Saul taught them. Acts also tells us very little about the complications and conflicts that can arise within a congregation as it seeks to know and do the will of Christ. To share an insider's view of both the process and the conflicts involved in seeking the Spirit, we may consult Paul's letters, especially those to the churches of Corinth and Galatia.

Or we can look at our own congregations. Some modern congregations are blessed by the outpouring of the Spirit, and, while the fruit of this outpouring may differ in significant ways from that first congregation in Jerusalem, the results look much the same: signs and wonders, faithful service, and contagious fellowship. Most of our Christian communities, though, more closely resemble Antioch's Christians-in-training than Pentecost Jerusalem. We are still striving to learn the tools and skills of discipleship, still listening for the Spirit's guidance. Luke's narrative in Acts and the issues addressed in the Epistles suggest that, despite our tendency to idealize the early church, very few congregations found their way to discipleship easily. Churches are more likely to learn to discern and follow the Spirit's guidance gradually than to receive the Spirit in full flood. Hearing the Spirit as a community has always required conscious effort and commitment. The fragmentation of community we experience today and the many distractions showered upon us by ubiquitous advertising and our cultural need to be constantly busy only make such effort and commitment more complicated and more necessary. Add in the human failings and spiritual entanglements we share with those whose stories we encounter in Scripture, and detours on our journey into discernment appear inevitable.

In this final chapter, I will reflect on some of the "speed bumps" we have hit at First United Methodist of Mount Sterling as we grow into the ministry of encouragement—particularly those bumps that have occurred in my months of writing this book—and the ways we have tried to stay faithful to the Spirit through them. I have borrowed the term "speed bumps" from Terry Tekyl's book *How to Pray After You Have Kicked the Dog*. He uses the term to describe difficulties or issues that arise in prayer, requiring us to stop and look honestly at how and why we are praying. Although they can be troublesome, speed bumps also provide a built-in opportunity for self-evaluation and can thus help us mature in prayer. I apply the term in a similar way to moments that have challenged and helped us evaluate our ministry at First UMC.

As you and your congregations explore the ministry of encouragement, you will probably have some of the same problems we did in adjusting to a new way of doing things—and problems appear even when we are not trying to do things a new way—but they will arise in contexts very different from ours at First. Having a clear idea of where we want to go and what we wish to accomplish in ministry does not ensure that we always practice ministry well, and the Spirit always has more to teach and new places to take us.

Speed Bumps

About six months ago, we were coming to the end of a lay council meeting. The final agenda item had to do with our goal of increasing the participation of laypeople in planning and leading worship. A further suggestion was made that this group would also look at the issue of whether it was time to add another worship service. There was no problem deciding that a short-term task force was better equipped than the whole council to handle these issues. Who would make up the new team? First one member of the council volunteered, then a couple who wished to add elements to our Sunday morning service that would result in "blended worship." The rest of the slots were quickly filled. Two weeks later the task force met. Only then did I realize that 10 of the 12 people on the new worship team already served on the lay council.

On the face of it, nothing was wrong with this situation. The people who wanted to do the work had volunteered and were ready to go. But some of us on the team saw red flags waving. We had not *invited* people outside the council into the process; we had *chosen* them—and not many of them. While we had tried to include a good cross-section of ages, interests, and lengths of membership, we were committing the old mistake of assuming that only those present or whose names occurred to us were available to do ministry. The leadership pool was not being enlarged—at least not by much—and the range of ideas was consequently limited. We were running the risk of becoming or being perceived as a leadership clique.

We had reverted to old habits. The previous structure of committees, councils, and boards was built on the assumption that ministry is done by the groups elected to do it. Outside help was sought only sporadically and pursued with little enthusiasm. Because the same people tended to get moved from committee to committee, the leadership pool remained small, and those outside the pool assumed that their ideas and participation were not needed. The result was rigidity in thinking and the limiting of opportunities for discipleship. Although I was already working on this book and the lay council had made it a priority to widen leadership within the congregation, we had together tumbled into the trap of habit. Habit was easier than thinking through other possibilities.

When these limitations were pointed out, I feared that we had just created a situation in which resentment could take root. By grace, the rest of the team also perceived the problem, so we began to talk about how we might reorganize the group. We used announcements in bulletin and newsletter to solicit names of people who might have interest in the team, and we made questionnaires available for the whole congregation to offer opinions on the direction worship might take. When we chose a team, we made certain the chair was someone not already on the council. We included representatives from the youth as well as the choir; we invited nonmusicians and both newer and longer-term members. When time came for the meetings, not all of the team participated equally (and some who had agreed to participate did not), but the opportunity for their participation and, therefore, for a real mix of ideas was there. The results have been as fraught with peril as all changes in worship can be; the expanded role of laity in leading prayers, reading Scripture, and preaching; the addition of contemporary music to what has become a "blended worship" service; and the discussion about beginning a second service—all have resulted in some raised eyebrows and much intense discussion. Still, the process itself has worked well.

I think it is not coincidental that this lapse into habit happened at a time when our focus on prayer had weakened. I have described in chapters 2 and 6 the emphasis on prayer that was essential to our discernment process. During the year and a half when we put this process in place, we had gathered in small groups—some meeting weekly, some monthly—to pray together for the ministry of the church. We held study groups on the practice of prayer and growth in prayer. I preached a series on the Lord's Prayer and emphasized prayer and the action of the Spirit as I preached through Acts. Perhaps we were not "prayer-soaked," but we had a pretty steady rain.

As we put the lay council in place, though, and began to address some of the goals our discernment had brought before us, things began to change. We became focused on the whats and hows of ministry, the nuts-and-bolts tasks of finding people and resources to accomplish our goals. As necessary as it is to attend to these details of ministry, I am sorry to say that our practice of communal prayer began to narrow. People tired of the weekly routine, perhaps, or felt that the prayer groups had become too rigid in keeping prayer for the church's ministries as a main focus. Some people dropped out. Some began to use our prayer groups as opportunities for planning or recruiting for ministry.

Our prayer studies shrank in number when our Disciple Bible Studies began. Although Disciple participants make a commitment to prayer, much of the class participants' prayer focus was on the needs and concerns of individuals in the church and community rather than specifically for the church's ministry. The prayer groups we had formed for such specific prayer also began to include personal needs and issues. I concur that prayer for individuals and their needs is vital, but the neglect of prayer for the ministry of the church had a noticeable effect. The process of praying for ministry is fairly simple, but it often takes a back seat in most churches (as it did again at First) to the needs of the ill and those in crisis. Prayer for ministry can be as simple as asking for the Spirit to keep our goals and focus as a church where God would have them. We also pray for specific ministries, the people who are involved in leading them, and those who are receiving them. If a ministry hits a problem or has trouble getting off the ground, we pray that it can be brought back on track, or that we may be led to discern what changes in direction or leadership God would have us make. Teaching about the importance of this kind of prayer is especially necessary in churches where "business" is traditionally isolated from "religion."

The old habits noted above are but one example of our new difficulties. But there were other signs. We experienced civil, but definite, dissension over our building renovation program. Disagreements arose over the administration of the community center. We even had a drop-off in the number of visitors to our worship. All these developments occurred over a period of six to 12 months and were all tied, I believe, to the subtle changes in the way we think of each other and treat each other that result when prayer is not the focus of the church. We have never expressed open hostility toward each other in or out of meetings— at least so far as I know—but an increase in minor carping and a decrease in the obvious joy and good humor that was so much a part of our fellowship during our discernment process affected us for these months.

Neglecting the power of prayer and falling into old habits are related, I believe, since it was prayer for guidance that moved us in our new direction in the first place. I think a third related factor was inadequately introducing people new to the congregation or to leadership to the ministry of encouragement. We assumed (one of the big sins of communication) that new participants in our ministry would understand what was happening just by becoming a part of it. This was simply not the case. People who joined First United Methodist in the past two years had not heard the sermon series on Acts that led me to the model of Barnabas and our congregation to the process of discernment. People who had joined in the past year not only missed that series; they also did not hear the sermon series on the Lord's Prayer and did not participate in our initial prayer studies. They were not part of the congregation when we formed the lay council and may not have understood its structure or the way it comes to a decision. They have been attracted to the spirit of welcome and support within the church that the ministry of encouragement has deepened, but they were not a part of the process that helped us grow and did not learn or understand the basis for the way we were doing ministry. We continued (and still continue) to attract and involve new families in our worship and ministry, thanks to God's grace and the good spirit within the congregation, but the time we can neglect the work of teaching and assimilation is past.

Contributing to the effect of these three factors was a lapse in pastoral leadership. The 18 months from November 2001 to May 2003 were a time of personal difficulty for me. Family discord led to sharp disagreements and severe financial stress that occupied my time, emotions, and attention to a harmful degree. These personal difficulties distracted me from my own ministry and were, at times, destructive of it. While writing this book has been helpful to my ministry and has been fulfilling to me personally, it ironically also distracted me at times from good practice of the encouragement that is the point of the book! While I take seriously the reality that the church's ministry is not my responsibility alone, my lack of leadership and distraction from God's call in those months hurt our work together at a critical time.

By God's grace, I caught the danger signs. I found myself angrier than appropriate at relatively minor problems arising in the church and on the Community Center board. I was again asking myself the questions about my fitness for ministry that I shared in chapter 4 ("fear of failing God"). Self-destructive feelings I thought I had set aside resurfaced. By God's grace, the support I needed was in place. I resumed seeing a counselor. I re-established the disciplines of prayer and Scripture reading noted in chapters 4 and 6. I shared what was happening and made myself accountable to my lay support team, one of whom responded by enlisting the Rebecca Circle of our United Methodist Women to surround me with a "prayer hedge." I spent time with my collegial support group and asked for their prayers. I made my district superintendent aware of the problem and accepted his advice and support. There is more conflict to work through and hard choices to come, but I believe I have the support I need to face them constructively and with integrity.

Remedies

As I wrote the first draft of this chapter, First Church began dealing with our speed bumps. The overall principle was simple—we had been on the right track before; we should return to that track. With this recognition, we embarked on an attempt to involve the whole congregation in rediscovering our vision for ministry. We actually began this process with a series of open meetings called "What's Going on at First Church?"

These meetings took place over four Sundays in summer 2002—twice for after-church potlucks and twice for late Sunday afternoon desserts. The approach was the same for all four meetings. Leaders of the lay council, the chair of the renovation team, those initiating the community center, and I met with whatever members chose to attend. Each leader made a brief presentation about the aspect of our ministry he or she represented, and we then invited comments and questions. Although the attendance was disappointing, it became clear that some were there to represent and test the waters on behalf of larger groups within the congregation. In every case, people who at the beginning of the meeting were hostile to the process or to a specific project learned enough to become supportive. One woman who had come with grave reservations even spoke in worship the Sunday after she attended the initial meeting, supporting our direction and ministries and urging other people with doubts to attend the remaining meetings to learn more. Of greater help to us, though, was the discovery that the ways we were communicating in our congregation were not working.

This discovery led us to a couple of new ideas. First, we began to insist that all Sunday announcements be written out and made available for insertion in the bulletin. Last-minute events or needs may be written out and posted on message boards outside the sanctuary. The intent was to help keep the focus of the service on worship, but it also required people to think ahead about what they wished to communicate and to make information available in a timely fashion. Writing out the message also lessened the possibility that the message would be misunderstood—a constant problem with oral announcements. Some resisted this requirement—thinking ahead, writing clearly, and being responsible are work, after all—and we still sometimes get announcements disguised as joys ("I am so glad we have the chance to have fellowship together at the potluck after church to benefit the youth work camp") and concerns ("I am really concerned that people might forget our scheduled ———— meeting Monday night"). The overall effect on worship, though, was positive. Beginning the service with music and prayer rather than updates and reminders keeps us more aware that our priority for that time really is worshiping God. And people have learned that the announcements page has information they need, not just items they have already heard.

Second, we planned an all-church retreat to review how and why we are doing ministry together. Here we reminded ourselves of the connection between prayer and discernment. We discussed the function of the lay council and invited comments and questions. We spoke about the changes our ministry has brought, whether they were experienced by the larger congregation in positive ways or negative, and how we might prepare for changes still to come. We invited all in attendance to share their dreams for the church's ministry, pledging to use those dreams as a guide to exploring possibilities for ministry in the coming year.

Along with these new ideas for communication came a new emphasis on communal prayer. Two new prayer groups began within the month—one on Tuesday evenings and one on Thursday mornings. We began by gathering at the community center rather than the church, hoping to involve people beyond our own congregation. When this did not happen and when participation was lower than we expected, we found that allowing the prayer groups to organize and connect as they wished—in person, by phone, or through e-mail—allowed us to involve more people than the original groups had. While we did and do attend to intercession for individuals in these groups, we also made plenty of space to pray for the ministry of our church and other churches in the community.

I also returned to the step I took at the beginning of this ministry and prayerfully invited a specific group of people to participate in gatherings. (The invitations were issued initially to those who were leaders in the church's ministry, but other names surfaced through my own time of prayer and through the suggestions of others.) Finally, I have committed to teach a Sunday morning class specifically aimed at helping people deepen their understanding and commitment to prayer. When demand arose for a similar class during the week, I set aside another commitment to make the class available. It was also suggested that I take us back through the book of Acts in a shortened sermon series to remind the congregation and ourselves as leaders what the ministry of encouragement can and should be.

All these were measures that took our attention back to our proper center. We began to focus less on what we think should come next or the direction we most want to go from here. We have recalled that what we have in mind for our congregation may or may not match what God has in mind. Instead we are again turning our attention to the process of prayer and discernment that brought our ministry alive in the first place. We trust that the Spirit will respond now as faithfully as in the past. Although those 18 months were challenging and even disappointing in some ways, there are enough signs of new growth and new direction that I am confident we are back on track.

Role of Preaching

Where does preaching fit into the ministry of encouragement? Clearly, our worship services give us access to the largest gathering of our congregation we are likely to have all week. As such, it gives us an opportunity to proclaim the message everyone needs to hear. The gospel is above all good news: "For God sent his Son into the world not to judge [condemn] the world, but so that through him the world might be saved" (John 3:17). This is the basic fact of salvation. In all our brokenness and sinfulness, God offers us another possibility. We were created for relationship with God and each other. God does confront us and judge us, but not to condemn. God's intent for us is repentance and healing, the joy and fullness of life we find together in Christ. The ministry of encouragement begins here. Prophetic words do need to be spoken, and sometimes the pulpit must become a place to confront misunderstanding or willful evil. But prophetic ministry is most effective when the reality of salvation has first been preached with conviction.

This is the starting point for preaching encouragement. But we also need to acknowledge that many of the people in our pews, longtime members as well as seekers, simply do not have a basic acquaintance with the scriptural message or a fundamental understanding of Christian faith. The enormous popularity of the Alpha Course[1] comes from this reality. Developed to introduce new Christians and seekers to Christian faith and doctrine, Alpha has become an educational phenomenon. Thousands of church members have attended. Worshipers' ignorance of Scripture and doctrine, which accounts for much of Alpha's popularity with committed Christians, means that the sermon can and must become a time of teaching.

One thing preachers can do to help overcome this illiteracy is to share with worshipers more of the exegetical work underlying the sermon—giving a helpful historical and social context of the Scripture and explaining a difficult word or ambiguous phrase. By doing so and by connecting the biblical story with our own, we help people to understand Scripture as a living text they can encounter personally and study for themselves. We can whet our congregation's appetite (perhaps creating a demand for an Alpha course or an intensive Bible study) to learn more about the basic ideas of faith—grace, repentance, the relationship between obedience and fullness of life, growth in faith. We have the opportunity to introduce members to what Dallas

Willard, professor of philosophy at the University of Southern California and author of several books on the traditional Christian disciplines, calls "the curriculum for Christlikeness"—exploring some of the basic skills of spiritual growth such as prayer, fasting, Bible study, sacrificial giving, and Christian fellowship (beyond the potlucks and social gatherings of the small groups described in chapter 4).[2]

I have already referred to the series I preached on the book of Acts during my first year at both Linden and First United Methodist. Such a series gives a congregation a chance to reflect together on a number of important issues—how the Holy Spirit is active in ministry, how the actions of "ordinary" Christians have great results, the "ripple effect" of sharing the gospel. It also allows us to ask questions about our own discipleship and sense of community in Christ. Other sermon series have been helpful to our common spiritual growth at First Church. A series on the Lord's Prayer mentioned above examined the prayer phrase by phrase and, supplemented by other Scripture about prayer, helped us learn how to use Christ's prayer as a model for our own. A sermon series on the Sermon on the Mount used Dallas Willard's book *The Divine Conspiracy* to look at this basic teaching by Christ not as an unattainable ideal but as practical instruction in nurturing a heart for discipleship. We also spent some time examining the ministry and theology of John Wesley, founder of Methodism, to see how his work—especially his emphasis on mutual accountability, means of grace, and social commitment—applies to us, his spiritual descendants.

While I have used the lectionary in the past, its limitations have led me to move away from it for extended periods. One cannot preach through Acts as the lectionary is currently set—or the Gospel of John or many of the prophetic writings from the Old Testament, for that matter. Passages from Acts are limited to the season after Easter, they are split among all three years of the lectionary cycle, and they are mostly excerpts from the sermons. The "plot" of Acts, the sense of the gospel's rippling movement from Jerusalem to Judea to the world, the growing awareness within the church that the gospel is bigger and more inclusive than even the apostles could guess—all these are lost by the lectionary. It is impossible to preach through the Sermon on the Mount as a unified whole in the lectionary. It skips "uncomfortable" parts altogether (such as Jesus' challenging words on divorce) and limits a crucial portion of Matthew 7 to those attending Ash Wednesday services. A multiweek examination of a spiritual discipline (prayer) or theological concept (the kingdom of God) can be very difficult to undertake when the lectionary is the only guide to sermon possibilities. The lectionary retains a place in my sermon planning and preparation, but even when following it, I find I often need to add verses to the ones selected to provide context or to avoid distortion of the less comfortable passages.

An important part of my sermon preparation is "sermon shaping." In this process, a group of laity—a different group is assigned each week of the month—meets with me for an hour each Monday to evaluate the sermon just preached and to study the passage for the following week. In the first half-hour, we examine the message the people heard in the previous sermon and the elements within the sermon or the service as a whole that helped or hampered their hearing of the message. On the positive side, participants may mention helpful illustrations or turns of phrase, a clear explanation of a theological term, or a well-placed hymn. On the negative side, they may cite an ill-fitting illustration, a jargon term, even a crying baby, or a sermon that went in an unexpected and thus distracting direction. The point is to determine whether the message I intended was the one heard and what expected or unexpected illumination took place. The second half-hour is used for exegesis on the passage to be preached the following Sunday. What is the central message? What is difficult to hear or needs clarification? What is the challenge to our lives as individual Christians or a community of Christ? How does the passage inspire growth or lead to discipleship?

This time has become invaluable to me in sermon preparation. I do not have to follow all, or any, of the paths of discussion we take during shaping, nor do I necessarily stick with the conclusions we draw during our conversation. The Spirit has something to say in this process, too. But sermon shaping ensures that I don't see the passage with only my own agenda in mind. It helps me hear the spiritual concerns of the congregation and the places where members (and I) need to grow and learn. It gives me insight into the correlation or gap between what we are doing in the sermon and what we do in other ministry. It keeps me from grinding my favorite axes over and over again. The people involved learn deeper Bible study and find themselves able to focus more on the real issues of the sermon. They also appreciate knowing that their thoughts have helped shape the sermon's direction, something I try to acknowledge within the sermon itself, as appropriate. Sermon shaping helps me preach better sermons and helps create better, helpfully critical listeners.

Barnabas, Our Mentor

Luke does not tell us what happened to Barnabas once he and Paul separated. We do not know where he traveled once he left for Cyprus; we don't know how long he worked for Christ, or his eventual fate. Barnabas' legacy is in the missionary work of Paul, a thriving and faithful congregation in Antioch, churches planted and tended on Cyprus, the ministry of John Mark (including, possibly, the first written gospel). We will not all be

Peters or Pauls or Wesleys or Luthers or, for that matter, founders of new megachurches; but Barnabas can still serve as mentor for most of us. Our legacy will be in the ministries of the churches we have served and those whose ministry we have stimulated and supported. May our ministries be as grace-full as that of our brother Barnabas.

NOTES

Preface

1. Eugene Peterson, *Under the Unpredictable Plant: An Exploration in Vocational Holiness* (Grand Rapids: Eerdmans, 1994).

2. Kennon Callahan, *Small, Strong Congregations: Creating Strengths and Health for Your Congregation* (San Francisco: Jossey-Bass, 2000), 12-13.

3. Callahan, *Small, Strong Congregations*, 15.

4. Kathleen Norris, *Dakota: A Spiritual Geography* (New York: Ticknor & Fields, 1993); *The Cloister Walk* (New York: Riverhead, 1996); *Amazing Grace: A Vocabulary of Faith* (New York: Riverhead, 1998).

5. Anne Lamott, *Operating Instructions: A Journal of My Son's First Year* (New York: Pantheon, 1993); *Bird by Bird: Some Instructions on Writing and Life* (New York: Pantheon, 1994); *Traveling Mercies: Some Thoughts on Faith* (New York: Pantheon, 1999).

6. Sam Williams, "Pastor's Progress," *Leadership* 21, no. 4 (Fall 2000): 32.

Chapter 1

1. Charles V. Bryant, *Rediscovering Our Spiritual Gifts: Building Up the Body of Christ Through the Gifts of the Spirit* (Nashville: Upper Room Books, 1991).

2. Bryant, *Rediscovering Our Spiritual Gifts*, 77.

3. Disciple Bible Study is a series of studies whose purpose is to develop Christian disciples and leaders through study of the Word.

Each study—there are now four—lasts from 32 to 34 weeks and requires a commitment of daily reading and reflection along with weekly group discussion. For more information, call the United Methodist Publishing House at (800) 672-1789, or go to its Web site at http://www.umph.org.

4. A helpful book for understanding this view of power in the church is Lovett H. Weems, Jr., *Leadership in the Wesleyan Spirit* (Nashville: Abingdon, 1999). See especially chapters 5 and 7.

Chapter 2

1. This issue of keeping the pastoral role as leader connected with the call to ministry is further explored in chapter 6.

2. John C. Harris, *Stress, Power, and Ministry* (Washington, D.C.: Alban Institute, 1977), 48-49, 57.

3. An adaptation of this covenant prayer is found in *The United Methodist Hymnal* (Nashville: United Methodist Publishing House, 1989); see 607, "A Covenant Prayer in the Wesleyan Tradition." The complete covenant service is in *The United Methodist Book of Worship* (Nashville: United Methodist Publishing House, 1992), 288-294. The full text of the prayer follows:

> I am no longer my own, but thine. Put me to what thou wilt, rank me with whom thou wilt. Put me to doing, put me to suffering. Let me be employed by thee or laid aside for thee, exalted for thee or brought low for thee. Let me be full, let me be empty. Let me have all things, let me have nothing. I freely and heartily yield all things to thy pleasure and disposal. And now, O glorious and blessed God, Father, Son, and Holy Spirit, thou art mine and I am thine. So be it. And the covenant I have made on earth, let it be ratified in heaven. Amen.

4. Since the apostle from Tarsus is referred to by both names in Acts, I will use both Saul and Paul, too. My practice will be to follow Luke's lead and use Saul or Paul, depending upon which passage of Acts is under discussion.

5. Some attention is paid in chapter 7 to the role of preaching in addressing this lack of understanding.

6. Weems, *Leadership in the Wesleyan Spirit*, 70.

Chapter 3

1. Disagreement prevails among New Testament scholars in regard to the precise meaning of the term "God-fearer." The details I present here are influenced by Howard Clark Kee, *To Every Nation Under Heaven: The Acts of the Apostles* (The New Testament in Context; Harrisburg, Pa.: Trinity Press International, 1997), especially 136-139; and Ben Witherington III, *The Acts of the Apostles: A Socio-Rhetorical Commentary* (Grand Rapids: Eerdmans; and Carlisle, Cumbria, U.K.: Paternoster Press, 1998), especially 341-344.

2. Bruce Malina, "Hospitality," *HarperCollins Bible Dictionary* (San Francisco: HarperCollins, 1996), 440.

3. Stephen Kliewer, *How to Live with Diversity in the Local Church* (Washington, D.C.: Alban Institute, 1987); and Roy M. Oswald and Speed B. Leas, *The Inviting Church: A Study of New Member Assimilation* (Washington, D.C.: Alban Institute, 1987).

Chapter 4

1. Harris, *Stress, Power, and Ministry*, 16-17 Although Harris should not be burdened with responsibility for the conclusions I draw in this chapter or in the book as a whole, his work has influenced my understanding of ministry greatly, and I am grateful for the help this book has given me over 20-odd years.

2. As an example of discovering alternatives, Weems (*Leadership in the Wesleyan Spirit*, 88-89) cites Wesley's synthesis of Calvinist theology, with its emphasis on the sovereignty and power of God, and Roman Catholic theology, with its emphasis on human responsibility and action. Wesley began by acknowledging God's sovereignty and the necessity of God's gracious action—action that reaches toward us before we are even aware of God. But he then continued by pointing to the necessity for humans to accept God's gift of grace and the need for us to respond to that gift through service and spiritual growth. Says Weems: "[Wesley's] task was not discovering new truths. It was looking at existing truths with a more open and integrative perspective."

Chapter 5

1. While I am aware that there is some doubt that Paul wrote the letters to Timothy, they do reflect the church's traditional belief that both Luke and Mark worked with Paul during his ministry.

2. The Emmaus Walk is a spiritual retreat derived from the Roman Catholic Cursillo movement. The Walk is intended to help Christians deepen their relationship with Christ and to discover how God might be calling them to servanthood. For more information or to find an Emmaus community located near you, go to the Web site http://www.upperroom.org/emmaus.

Chapter 6

1. These reminders and complaints form a commentary on the prophet's work and are often called Jeremiah's Confessions. They are a source of challenge and comfort during difficult times in ministry. The relevant passages are Jeremiah 11:18–12:6; 15:10-21; 17:14-18; 18:18-23; and 20:7-18.

2. Eugene Peterson, *Working the Angles: The Shape of Pastoral Integrity* (Grand Rapids: Eerdmans, 1987), 2.

3. Peterson, *Working the Angles*, 2.

4. This is not to suggest that those who step out of ordained ministry are spiritual failures. Sometimes it is attentiveness to God's call that leads us out of ordained ministry and into a new and equally faithful way of serving God. Not all who are called to ordained ministry are intended to spend their entire working lives as pastors. When people come later in life to ordained ministry, we dignify them with the phrase "second-career pastors." However, when the vocational transition is reversed, with people leaving active ordained ministry for another calling, we too often assume they have failed in their "real" calling. Though perhaps natural, this assumption is unfortunate, if not mean-spirited. This negative response to people who follow God's call to a ministry beyond the ordained status may also come from the continued unscriptural—and snobbish—elevation of the ordained ministry above the ministry of the laity, an attitude that continues to be deplored within the church as widely as it continues to be practiced.

Chapter 7

1. The Alpha Course was developed by Charles Maraham, an Anglican priest looking for a way to introduce new Christians to the basic principles of the faith. Constructed as a series of dinners and

informal talks, Alpha has become an effective evangelism tool, bringing thousands into their first relationship with Christ. Alpha's Web site is http://www.alphacourse.org.

2. Willard explores this need as a part of his work on the Sermon on the Mount in *The Divine Conspiracy: Rediscovering Our Hidden Life in God* (San Francisco: Harper San Francisco, 1998), 311-373. His exploration should be read and reread—as should the whole book—by pastors concerned with the process of making disciples.

RECOMMENDED READING

Bryant, Charles V. *Rediscovering Our Spiritual Gifts: Building Up the Body of Christ through the Gifts of the Spirit.* Nashville: Upper Room Books, 1991.
Bryant's book contains a helpful description of the spiritual gifts listed by the apostles Paul and Peter. In his introduction to the gifts, he is careful to emphasize that each has importance, and he gives excellent examples of the ways each gift might be used within a congregation. He includes a useful spiritual-gifts inventory for use by individuals or congregations.

Callahan, Kennon. *Small, Strong Congregations: Creating Strengths and Health for Your Congregation.* San Francisco: Jossey-Bass, 2000.
As with all of Callahan's work, he offers plenty of practical advice for discovering and making the best use of your congregation's strengths. I admit, however, that a large part of this book's attraction for me was the church-growth guru's affirmation that small churches are capable of vital, exciting ministries.

Foster, Richard. *Prayer: Finding the Heart's True Home.* San Francisco: HarperSanFrancisco, 1992.
Foster is probably better known for *Celebration of Discipline,* a modern classic, but I make more use of this work in my teaching and preaching. I find it less directive and more invitational than its predecessor, and I believe that it helps all

135

who use it to discover the realm of prayer as a much larger and more varied world than they had imagined.

Harris, John C. *Stress, Power, and Ministry.* Washington, D.C.: Alban Institute, 1977.
This is one of my two desert-island books, along with Dallas Willard's. I have read it every three or four years for the entire 20-plus years I have been a pastor, and I am always encouraged, challenged, and strengthened by its insights. Harris gives a realistic view of the structures and currents of power within a congregation and between church and judicatory. In doing so, he alerts us to the pastor's need to develop a sense of healthy autonomy. Harris's prescription for autonomy has helped shape my understanding of authenticity.

Kee, Howard Clark. *To Every Nation Under Heaven: The Acts of the Apostles.* The New Testament in Context. Harrisburg, Pa.: Trinity Press International, 1997.
Although this is a solid, scholarly work, it is blessedly free of jargon. Kee deals clearly and informatively with the social and cultural world in which the church of Acts took root and grew. Several times I found myself reading much further in the text than research required.

Kliewer, Stephen. *How to Live with Diversity in the Local Church.* Washington, D.C.: Alban Institute, 1987.
In this helpful book, Kliewer assumes that all congregations have levels of diversity and that diversity can be either a creative or a destructive force. He provides a clear and logical method for facing diversity and conflict in the local congregation.

Oswald, Roy M., and Speed B. Leas. *The Inviting Church: A Study of New Member Assimilation.* Washington, D.C.: Alban Institute, 1987.
This work does much more than the title promises. Oswald and Leas demonstrate that the personality of a congregation counts for more than formal programs or committees in attracting and keeping new church members ("less indoctrination—more contagion"). They also provide tools for self-assessment that help a congregation ask, What type of congregation are we? How do we welcome and include (or

how do we exclude) new people? I have found that this work also helps congregations evaluate how people become inactive and to devise healthy ways to invite inactive members to return.

Peterson, Eugene H. *Under the Unpredictable Plant: An Exploration in Vocational Holiness.* Grand Rapids: Eerdmans, 1992.
Peterson turns to the story of the prophet Jonah to explore the meaning of vocation. Although the book is intended for clergy, the underlying themes of vocational holiness and the holiness of the ordinary will be helpful to all who read it.

————. *Working the Angles: The Shape of Pastoral Integrity.* Grand Rapids: Eerdmans, 1987.
Peterson's deep feelings about the need for pastoral integrity are evident in this book as he speaks strongly against the captivity to nonessentials many pastors accept. For Peterson, prayer, study of Scripture, and spiritual direction are not just support systems for pastoral ministry—they are the core of ministry. His pages on the Psalms are particularly effective.

Tekyl, Terry. *How to Pray After You've Kicked the Dog,* Muncie, Ind.: Prayer Point Press, 1999.
Tekyl has written a practical, accessible guide to personal prayer that has a welcome touch of humor. The final section, a look at the various "temperaments" of prayer, invites the reader to develop a style of prayer that speaks to the reader's own personality and need.

————. *Pray the Price.* Muncie, Ind.: Prayer Point Press, 1997.
Probably more than any other book, this one opened my eyes to the need for and power of congregational prayer. Tekyl also goes beyond the church walls to challenge churches to transform their entire communities through acts of prayer. This work is thought-provoking and full of specific suggestions for energizing a congregation.

Weems, Lovett H., Jr. *Leadership in the Wesleyan Spirit.* Nashville: Abingdon, 1999.
Weems returns to the roots of John Wesley's reform movement and applies them to the work of Wesley's modern

successors. Although intended to help in the renewal of the Wesleyan family of denominations, several principles Weems invokes—focusing on service, remembering the poor, creative use of conflict, and the necessity for spiritual growth, among others—cross denominational boundaries.

Willard, Dallas. *The Divine Conspiracy: Rediscovering Our Hidden Life in God.* San Francisco: HarperSanFrancisco, 1998.
Along with Harris's work, this book is my absolute "must read." Willard confronts the church's reluctance to challenge people to live a life of genuine discipleship or to teach them that discipleship is a necessary component of full life. His words are not just a polemic; throughout the book, but particularly in the pages I cite in chapter 7, Willard gives practical advice on how to alert our congregations that the "kingdom of God is at hand."

Witherington, Ben III. *The Acts of the Apostles: A Socio-Rhetorical Commentary.* Grand Rapids: Eerdmans; and Carlisle, Cumbria, U.K.: Paternoster Press, 1998.
This is an exhaustive look at Acts, containing more material than nonspecialists would normally use. Still, I found several helpful nuggets in the course of my reading, and, given the scope of the book, Witherington has done everything possible to make his work accessible to the general reader.